D0229576

Lincolnshire
COUNTY COUNCIL

COMMUNITIES, CULTURAL SERVICES
and ADULT EDUCATION
**This book should be returned on or before
the last date shown below.** DS16

	DEC 4. 13	23 JUL 2014
10 DEC 2009		20 AUG 2014
		13 OCT 2014
18 FEB	24. MAY	
05 JUL 11.		
24. AUG 11.	01. 07. 13	
19. SEP 11.		
	29. 07. 13.	
27. JUN 12	29. OCT 13.	
03. DEC 12.	19 FEB 2014	
10 JAN 2013	20 MAY 2014	
	10 JUN 2014	

To renew or order library books please telephone 01522 782010
or visit www.lincolnshire.gov.uk
You will require a Personal Identification Number.
Ask any member of staff for this.

EC. 199 (LIBS): RS/L5/19

04532643

Will's

Shooting Ways

Will's
Shooting Ways
Days with pen, brush and gun

Quiller

Lincolnshire County Council	
AD 04532643	
Askews	
799.294	£25.00
	0917989/0082

Copyright © 2009 Will Garfit

First published in the UK in 2009
by Quiller, an imprint of Quiller Publishing Ltd

British Library Cataloguing-in-Publication Data
A catalogue record for this book
is available from the British Library

ISBN 978 1 84689 036 9

The right of Will Garfit to be identified as the author of this work has been asserted in accordance with the Copyright, Design and Patent Act 1988.

The information in this book is true and complete to the best of our knowledge. All recommendations are made without any guarantee on the part of the Publisher, who also disclaims any liability incurred in connection with the use of this data or specific details.

All rights reserved. No part of this book may be reproduced or transmitted in any form or by any means, electronic or mechanical including photocopying, recording or by any information storage and retrieval system, without permission from the Publisher in writing.

Book and jacket design by Sharyn Troughton

Printed in China

Quiller

An imprint of Quiller Publishing Ltd
Wykey House, Wykey, Shrewsbury, SY4 1JA
Tel: 01939 261616 Fax: 01939 261606
E-mail: info@quillerbooks.com
Website: www.countrybooksdirect.com

*This book is dedicated to my father who opened the
door onto the countryside just wide enough for me to
jump through and find joy in all around me: its
beauty, wildlife, people and sports all nurtured a
passion which has become such an important
part of my life and for which I am
forever grateful.*

Contents

Foreword

It was in 1986 that I first visited Hauxton on a shoot day. It was memorable for lots of reasons, not least of which being that the first bird shot was a towering woodpigeon which fell to the first barrel of Archie Coats' gun.

Hauxton is of course the Laurent Perrier Award winning oasis of a shoot and fishery which Will created from 70 acres of disused mineral workings. It is stunning and truly the work of an artist. So how appropriate in this setting to see a key early mentor bring down a sporting quarry which was such a passion for both of them.

When, 10 years later, my *Gazette* pigeon shooting columnist disappeared from his hide, I put in a call to Will. Our paths had crossed many times over the years, almost always in agreeable circumstances; Will also provided some lovely illustrations for my book *The Game Shot*. It was abundantly clear that he had more to offer than most on the subject – and he is a premier league shot. I ghosted the first two or three articles, before Will suggested that he might like to have a go. So often when people write for a publication for the first time they seem to think they have to put words together in a way which is alien to them. Not Will. From the outset he wrote as if painting. These were Will's letters or extended notes and thoughts for his gamebook and were published intact (once the handwriting had been deciphered!).

Pigeon shooting was to prove the thrust of the column, but all manner of subjects were to be covered. Mostly with a story to tell or a point to make in the nicest way possible, he has now put together some 150 columns, from which selected pieces have yielded a fascinating book.

By profession Will is a river artist, and an exceedingly good one. Obviously gifted and trained, he also has a very perceptive eye which has been so instrumental in his writings. He can always find something different and interesting to say. His participation in the Countryside March, for instance, led to on-page musings about range judging... pigeons flying around Nelson's Column at 157 feet would be safe from all but George Digweed and Richard Faulds! On the subject of high birds and range, he puts it succinctly elsewhere when he says: 'We want birds which can produce thrilling shooting and can be killed cleanly within our own capabilities with a gun we enjoy using.' Perfect.

In this book we share many happy hours with him in a pigeon hide as well as travels elsewhere in pursuit of all manner of game. It is both a thoughtful and entertaining read – I'm sure you'll enjoy it.

Mike Barnes
Editor
Fieldsports

Introduction

How on earth did I get into writing. I am an artist. Having spent seven years at art school, I paint and illustrate the landscape and the countryside sports I enjoy. However, like many people, my life evolved in a mysterious way, almost by accident.

So it was with my writing. One day in 1996, Mike Barnes, the founder and editor of *Shooting Gazette*, telephoned me to enquire if I knew where a mutual pigeon shooting friend, Jim, had gone as his article for the following month was overdue. A week later the same but more urgent query, again I could not help. It was then that Mike suggested I cover for him - it was easy Mike assured me. He would ask me questions relating to an aspect of pigeon shooting and then he would write the piece based on my answers. With my passion for pigeon shooting this indeed was not difficult and a few moments thought about the enigmatic bird and the exciting sport it produces can get me chatting for hours. So it came to pass that for two or three months, with still no sign of Jim, I found myself the pigeon shooting correspondent without having actually written a word!

Then I started to create ideas and for one article, which had a number of names and facts, it seemed easier to write a rough draft. Mike immediately phoned to say if I could write like that he would pay me double (think pence not pounds – neither artists nor writers retire – they just die of old age). Twelve years and several editors later here we are with some 150 articles from which to select this anthology. Each editor still inherits me and my hand-written monthly offering on lined A4 paper spat onto his desk from a fax machine. It is a good discipline once a month to focus on an incident or story and sit in the garden in summer or by the fire in winter, and scribble a few words.

Actually, three years earlier, having won the Laurent Perrier Award (now the Purdey Award) for my game and conservation project, I was approached to write a book of the story. The publisher asked in what style did I write? Never having written a book before I replied that it would not be in high prose but I was comfortable to write as if it was a letter to a friend. He suggested I send a first chapter to him which he would forward to his editor. She was an Oxford University literary lady of distinction. As I waited for a response I felt as if I was back at school awaiting damning criticism for my last essay from the English master. A short reply from her, 'Yes, she could work with my English.' I was flattered that she had said 'with' not 'on'. I later realised it was a diplomatic and kind way of achieving the latter.

The following year *Will's Shoot* was published (republished in 2005 as *Will's Shoot Revisited*). I was painting commissions on the Isle of Lewis in the Outer Hebrides. Ted Hughes, at that time the Poet Laureate, was there in the fishing party.

I cringed as our mutual friend introduced me and mentioned I had just had my book published. (Rather like being introduced to Schumacher or Lewis Hamilton as a man who drives an old Land Rover.) However later I did have a fascinating conversation with the great literary man about the creative writing process and he encouragingly said he always wrote his poems and books in long-hand on A4 pads. I mention this to editors who suggest I write on a 'word processor' and e-mail articles to them as an 'attachment'. Sorry but I paint on site, whatever the weather, up mountain or down dale and write in the fresh air where I can feel the wind on my face as I describe a pigeon coming in to the decoys.

Over the years I am becoming more sensitive about statistics, particularly those relating to big bags. However, as all my earliest shooting was alone with a .410 wandering the fields and hedgerows around our village, with very few opportunities of a shot, I kept a very personal game diary. This recorded the odd rat, squirrel or pigeon stalked or surprised on my travels and I kept a column for the shots I had expended. I have always had a fascination for statistics and so have continued to keep a personal record and game diary. When my first articles appeared it was acceptable to lay out a big bag of pigeons and tell the story of the day. Later it became important that there should be a story of which a good bag was incidental – not the subject of that story. There is no threat to the woodpigeon population and the sport of shooting them is subject to one's field craft, experience and skill. A big bag is earned and pigeon shooting, whilst being sport for the shooter, is also effective crop protection for the farmer. It is a wild bird and the number one avian agricultural pest. So a strange symbiotic relationship develops as while the farmer hates pigeons the genuine pigeon shooter loves and respects them as his sporting quarry.

We are all interested in fact and figures whether illustrating highs or lows of a situation – either can be embarrassing at times. The truth is that over the years I have found that my most memorable articles recalled by readers are those when everything has gone wrong on the day for me!

As Mike Barnes got me into this, I felt it appropriate to invite him to write the Foreword. We remain good friends and I am most grateful to him not only for his kind words but for that challenge and opportunity to write a monthly article to share my experiences of sporting days, alone in a pigeon hide or in the company of those who make the day and enrich the joy of shooting. May we, and those who come after, continue to enjoy days out shooting long into the future.

Pigeon Perfect

I spent an enjoyable day in a pigeon hide with arguably the country's best shot and current holder of the pigeon shooting record – George Digweed.

It was with some apprehension that I had looked forward to this. Rather like being on the front row of the grid next to Schumacher or partnering Borg at tennis.

George had just returned from South Africa as FITASC World Champion for the third time whilst I'd arrived home chuffed to bits with a bottle of port won at the CLA stand at the Game Fair.

So here we were, as guests of Phil Beasley, dropped on a rape stubble and left to get on with it, whilst he took two American clients elsewhere. Actually I felt it was with his customary sense of humour that he'd lit the blue touch paper of an explosive double firework and stood back out of danger! The blue in George's big bang was his Digweed Royal Blues, a 35 gm cartridge loaded by Kent Cartridge Company, having been developed for long range performance. The blue in Phil's case was his colourful language!

George shot with his 32" barrelled Kemen choked full and full. I had my Spanish side-by-side, 28" barrels bored ¼ and ¾ and used Gamebore 30 gm 'Clear Pigeon'.

We watched the field, actually two adjacent fields with a hedge between, and both agreed on the way we read the situation from pigeons we saw feeding and flying about. We decided to shoot from the middle hedge but about a hundred yards from the belt of trees at the far end. Our cars were used strategically to prevent pigeons settling at the other end of the two fields. These, with the noise of shots, would hopefully keep birds moving upwind to us.

Soon we discovered a big difference in approach to hide building. George likes an open-topped 360 degree visibility hide whilst I prefer one with a tall background and a partial top to the rear half. This prevents birds spotting me if they come from behind before turning into the decoys. He prefers to have full vision and stands all the time whilst I shoot sitting down.

So we built two hides together parted by one camouflage net. We used foliage to soften the effect and set out our fifteen dead birds as decoys. We agreed on this and had them in two groups about 20 yards out from the hide. Incoming pigeon would hopefully come to the gap in front of our hide between the groups. I was surprised that George agreed with the idea of decoys placed comparatively close in considering the range he can shoot. However, we have the same philosophy – you can always take them further out or make more rights and lefts but if the decoys are far out, you don't have so many options to increase your chances.

Now how would we operate together? Would I even get a shot? It soon became clear that I am happy to take on anything up to 50 yards but that is the sensible limit of my game gun. But George has the skills and power of shot to kill birds out to 80 yards – yes, 80 yards. He suggested that I take anything which came inside my range and he'd take anything, passing by over or beyond 50 yards. 'One for the popgun', he'd say as a bird came to the decoys and he left it for me. If two came we did a synchronised shooting trick of me taking the left and he the right. When on occasion three or four came then again, a flurry of shots and the sky was clear but for feathers drifting away on the breeze.

The system worked 'perfect' as George said and I was interested to see just how gentlemanly and generous he was. In fact I've seldom found it easier to shoot with anyone sharing a hide. The vital thing, of course, is safety and I would always advocate making two adjacent single hides rather than one big one, so each Gun has a clearly defined shooting area and angle.

Toby, George's black lab, was an experienced campaigner with his nose pressed to the netting at the front of the hide, marking long, winged birds. A gruff 'go on' from George and Toby was off like a whippet, usually straight to the bird. If he needed redirecting when out, then a whirring of arms, two-fingered whistles and shouts of 'Go back you bugger' or other well chosen phrases, were all registered by Toby as an encouragement to do his own thing. People queue for George's shooting masterclasses but I suspect his dog training classes are less well attended! Nevertheless, Toby usually found the pigeon and returned exhausted to the hide more for a drink of water than to deliver the bird to hand.

However, what was incredible was George's shooting technique and I can see how he achieved his record bag. It begins with exceptional eyesight as he spots pigeon before they appear as dots on the horizon to a normal eye and he can identify stock dove from woodpigeon at a range before most people would first see it was a bird at all. So then he's ready in his open-topped hide. On this particular day they were decoy and hide-shy so just passed by, giving long rangy shots. However, when within 70–80 yards he would shoot the birds with amazing consistency.

I asked him what he focused upon when shooting such birds. Was it lead, speed or line? 'Line is everything', he said, 'squirt far enough ahead and the shot string will take care of lead – but if it's not on line, there's no chance'. He seemed allergic to birds within 50 yards but where a normally competent shot finishes, George Digweed starts.

What did surprise me was that he did not wear hearing protection – George, while you can still hear, listen to the good advice and look at all the deaf old codgers you meet. I'd hate you to miss my shout of 'good shot' if we should enjoy a day together again.

It was not a big day as the lines faded and pigeon found quieter fields in which to feed. However, the lulls gave us time to chat about the shooting world in general and not just about his top class clay competitions but also about game shooting, which is really George's great love – not heady numbers days but the quality high birds of the Devon shoots, flighting teal or making a mixed bag on the Romney Marshes.

On normal game shoots he is a victim of his own success and often finds himself in a no-win situation. If he leaves birds he doesn't consider sporting, his host and keeper say: 'How do we give him a shot?' If he kills everything, they and fellow Guns claim there's nothing left for the rest of the season. If he were to miss, they'd never stop pulling his leg and laughing. Instead of being thrilled to admire and acknowledge a unique shot of world class, he becomes resented in a cloud of jealousy, notably on the competition circuit. Here is a man who respects his quarry, is a good naturalist, understands the country and shoots with a high standard of ethics. His problem is that he's just too good a shot. He's often driven to think he'd rather be alone in a hedgerow with his dog and the chance of shooting fifteen or twenty pigeon.

In any other country he'd be a national hero and household name but for some reason British world clay pigeon shooting champions are only known by those who venture between the covers of the shooting press. The man's a legend in his own time and I enjoyed sharing the day – while a three-figure bag was not forthcoming, the sixty pigeon picked gave us sport enough and memories which will live on.

Delights and Frustrations of Pigeon Roost Shooting

February is a month when many of us go woodpigeon shooting but relatively few pigeon are actually shot. The reason for this is that it is not so much pigeon shooting, but shooting at pigeons.

We are talking about roost shooting: getting under the flight lines as the birds go back to the woods to roost. It is probably the most difficult and testing of all types of shooting but its appeal is irresistible. Undoubtedly it is more social than any other form of pigeon shooting, but when the wind is in the right direction, you've got under a flight line and the whole exercise works, then it is also the most brilliant sport.

The problem invariably lies in the weather – there are all too few wild windy days. Instead we have still February afternoons, when the birds are easily spooked and soon take to flying at impossible heights.

But, even when the conditions are less than perfect, there is still a chance of having some decent sport. As with any form of woodpigeon shooting, reconnaissance can hold the key. Try, during the previous day or so, to have a good look at the wood that you are going to be shooting. Hopefully you will see where the birds are flying, and where they are mostly pitching into.

Sometimes, if you stand back and watch you can also see their exit point from a wood. This can be useful as, when Guns start shooting, the birds may decide to move to another wood.

Another thing to watch for is obvious pigeon droppings at the foot of what is clearly a roosting tree. In fact a particular tree, such as a tall ash, might well be a focal point at which the pigeon aim when they flight into the wood at night. You really have to be aware of what is happening – even if installed into an apparently good position, if the birds change their flight then be prepared to move. Don't just stand there waiting for something to happen.

Ideally you will pick a spot which gives good concealment, but with a window above you amongst the branches, through which you will be able to see and shoot. When pigeon are approaching I tend to hold the gun three-quarter mounted so that minimum movement is needed when I actually take the shot.

The most important thing is to make every shot count. On Saturday afternoons in February most woods are manned as part of a co-ordinated effort to raise funds for the Game and Wildlife Conservation Trust. This stems back to the time when there was a National Pigeon Day, aimed at reducing the flocks of woodpigeons before their onslaught into the spring crops.

So, bearing in mind that other people are also looking for some shooting, take only those birds which are clearly within range. Don't be tempted much over treetop height. The average tree is 60–80 feet high. If you go 20–30 feet above that then we are talking about a very difficult shot. Pheasants at such a height are testing, but pigeon with their unpredictable and misleading flight are incredibly difficult. Such shots are not only a waste of good cartridges, they may well be spoiling sport for others.

Don't worry about not shooting. This will give the birds the confidence to come in lower. If you start blasting away on the edge of range however, you will only succeed in sending them ever upwards.

Keeping concealed is very important. Position yourself as much out of sight as possible – an ivy clad tree (or fallen tree) is often a good point from which to shoot. Or, if you find a thorn tree or bush, you can position yourself well hidden, but able to see oncoming pigeon through the branches.

I always keep my head well down and look up from under the peak of my cap. A glimpse of your face and a pigeon is easily spooked, even at extreme range. If you have some gloves it might help, and I am sure masks too are a bonus, though I tend not to use one myself. The whole idea is to keep movement at a minimum.

I have found lofting decoys to be quite effective. I will loft a decoy (dead pigeon) in a cradle onto the downwind side of a tree. I use an ordinary cradle, jammed into the top of a lofting pole. Elastic bands hold the bird in position. By accident I discovered that if the wings are broken and hanging loose it tends to work rather better. When the wind gets under the decoy's wings it looks like a settling bird.

However, roost shooting is the one form of pigeon shooting where one needs no decoys or toys. With just a gun and cartridges, on a windy evening, a wood can produce the most exhilarating sport.

It's No Coincidence

Cocks only

As the game shooting season moves into top gear it is time to reflect and consider what connection there is between pigeon and game shooting.

In my area of East Anglia all the stubbles have gone and the horizon is wall-to-wall winter wheat, lush young rape or deep-ploughed winter beans.

Yes, there are some good pigeon days to be had but most pigeon shooters become involved in the game season one way or another, maybe beating or picking up for keeper friends on whose area they enjoy the sport with pigeons at other times of the year. Many farms become no-go areas prior to and during the game season for fear of disturbance to game.

What game birds find disturbing is someone on the move. I find there is no disturbance to game from pigeon shooting from a fixed position. Pheasants and partridges soon potter about, feeding even, amongst the decoys whilst shooting is taking place.

Nevertheless, one must sympathise with the keeper who has enough problems rearing and nurturing game through the summer for a few days shooting in the winter. It's one more hassle he can do without whilst ensuring all goes smoothly.

Most pigeon shooters get a chance to shoot game at some stage of the season and I would back them to perform above average, if not exceptionally well. It is no coincidence that three of the best game shots I've known, Archie Coats, John Ransford and George Digweed, have each held the record for woodpigeon bags.

There are a number of good reasons for this. An obvious one is that pigeon shooters keep their eye in all the year, unlike many game shots whose guns stay securely locked in gun cabinets from February until the first grouse, partridge or pheasant day dawns several months later.

The pigeon shooter has honed his technique to tackle his quarry flying at any speed, angle or height. This has often been in a cramped hide, possibly seated, often with poor visibility to ensure he remains hidden behind leafy screen or camouflaged net. If he can perform well in such circumstances, just think how much easier it is to shoot in the open where there is ample time for footwork and unhurried gun mounting. There is more time to see and address the pheasant or partridge and, above all, these game birds do not jink away like a pigeon but either fly on a predetermined line or, at worst, veer on a gentle arc.

'Hang on' you say – that makes game shooting look so simple for a pigeon shooter. No shot is easy, pigeon, game or clay until you've hit it. Often what look to be the most straightforward shots are those most easily missed. The wonderful challenge and ultimate excitement of game shooting is that each species can produce the easiest and also the most testing and difficult shots.

The first grouse I shot drifted past like a decoyed pigeon, making far from difficult shooting. I'd heard so much about the challenge of driven game; how strange, I thought – until the next drive which was downwind. Birds that were as big as brown hens in the previous drive became jet-propelled bees, no sooner in sight than gone away over the heather knoll behind.

For better or for worse, most partridge shooting is now of reared French partridges. These can give wonderful sport in country with the right topography or on flat ground using the wind.

I love the variety of days with a mixture of partridges and pheasants. The buzz to be had from one or two special shots will produce memories of the sport that will live on and on. However, for pure adrenaline nothing can compare with grouse driven downwind over a butt with a short skyline. All our game birds have their own character and provide challenging sport. I come back to the fact that a pigeon shooter will be well equipped mentally and physically to rise to this challenge. He will benefit from his experience and his fieldcraft will ensure that he fully enjoys the richness of the day in the countryside.

There is a two-way benefit of game shooting – it can bring further experience to the all-round shot and thus enhance the performance of the pigeon shooter on his next day's decoying.

The Big Day

All the hard work has paid off... it's helpers' day on my award winning shoot at Hauxton in Cambridgeshire.

After the four main days before Christmas I organise the helpers' day in early January. On most shoots the beaters' day is right at the end of the season but at Hauxton all those who assist are close friends who help throughout the year in so many ways with other activities. For

years Reg has been a fantastic help with tree work, road maintenance, hedge cutting or whatever. His brother, Philip, provides a ton or two of corn surplus after seed trials. John Barnard has always been there at the 'drop of a hat' if there is any work or problem with the fisheries. Peter Elliott, an old friend who has built up a very successful fruit farming enterprise over the road, has helped for years with trees, security, machinery or whatever. Young James, son of Bob the rat man, takes over feeding when the rest of us go to Scotland to walk up grouse in Invernesshire.

The helpers' day team of some dozen or so friends included of course Roger and Brian who have actually been involved for quite a number of years. As the team seldom have the opportunity of much shooting I like to have their day when there is still sufficient game about for everyone, hopefully, to get some sport.

It has become known as 'the big day'. This relates more to the number of guns than the size of the bag but it is the most special day of the season for everyone involved. There are normally fourteen guns. Carl and Roger were unable to beat so they stood at each drive, the others are split into two teams who beat and stand alternately. For safety reasons the beating team are not armed and this also prevents any confusion or accusation as to whether a bird flushed was going forward over the standing guns or back over the beaters! I try to share the better potential drives and the lesser ones. One problem is, of course, that there are only half the beaters, dogs or stops for each drive compared with a normal day and some pheasants 'tuck in' or 'run out' and so avoid the guns. However, there are usually birds in every drive and the standard of the shooting is very accurate especially considering how few opportunities many of them have to go pheasant shooting in a season.

After these manoeuvres some guns go to the Everglades to flight pigeons whilst the remainder drain the last coffee from their flasks before manning the hides around the Lodge Lake to flight the duck. Later still, just as the flight is ending, there is sometimes the distant sound of sporadic honking and a minute later Canada geese circle and drop in to offer the last shots of the day.

Geese often produce the highlight shot of someone's day. However, I always ask Guns not to shoot the greylags as numbers are not yet sufficient. One day, as a mallard flew upwind high over Bob, he upped his gun and with a mighty swing killed it cleanly. However, simultaneously a greylag passed over, going downwind in the opposite direction, from behind, and apparently flew into the shot. Those who witnessed the event, of course, made much of the demise of the forbidden goose which Bob swore he never ever saw but he was christened 'Greylag Bob' nevertheless!

My son, Henry, feels he is not eligible to shoot unless he's helped beating with the team on the preceding shoot day which used to be at the beginning of his school holidays. As a teenager he shot his first pheasant and in fact got two in the same drive, both good crossers high over the trees on the corner of the Everglades. I don't know who was the more thrilled, him or me standing with him, a very proud father. That day's other highlight was when Terry, the policeman, let out a surprised cheer as he shot two mallard, his first ever right and left. He has never claimed to be a great shot but to wait until his mid-fifties to achieve this does show considerable patience! Well done Terry!

At the end of the helpers' day a typical bag could be thirty-five pheasants, eighteen mallard, two tufted duck, three moorhen, two rabbits (caught by dogs), twenty-four pigeon, two woodcock, three Canada geese, one snipe, one magpie and one squirrel (probably after four shots). So a total of perhaps ninety-two head after a very sporting day.

This is followed by an enormous meal at home when, with three tables set at angles like dominoes across the kitchen, we can sit up to eighteen packed in tight, shoulder to shoulder. Reg will carve two loaves of bread into one inch steps while I serve Gina's legendary cottage pie with a brown crispy top, steaming from the oven. A big square dish serves six proper portions.

These are hungry lads after a long day's shoot. A chockie pud of some sort is always popular to follow after which, with the port and cheese, Bob announces the result of the day's sweepstake. Then I take the opportunity to say a few words to thank all for their help throughout the season. The day is a climax of the year's teamwork and I cannot help being rather repetitive each year on this occasion, pointing out how it could not work without the support, help and goodwill of all present.

Mark, being the most senior, would usually respond on their behalf with a few kind words about how they have all enjoyed the day and everything at Hauxton, whether work or sport during the year.

Bob very kindly presents Gina with an enormous plant or colossal box of fruit for which they have all contributed – a very touching gesture and much appreciated.

What a wonderful thing it is to enjoy a day's sport with friends.*

Later in January there are three more shoots. A day for chums run as a full day, then two further forays with about half a dozen key helpers all shooting. Two may stand as forward guns while the others drive the cover with dogs. These days are always a lot of fun and quite successful, as we drive many of the woods in the reverse direction to normal, which tends to catch out cocks that have learned to avoid the guns.

All three last days are followed by the pigeon and duck flights. Again the geese may arrive late offering the last shot of a sporting day to produce a very mixed bag.

*Sadly some of these friends are no longer with us.

JUDGING RANGE

How good are we at judging range of birds flying high over us? This was the question I addressed whilst milling about waiting for the first Countryside March to start. I was there with a car load of mates and enjoyed meeting people from far and wide, drawn together in the common cause to support the countryman's interest in the countryside. What an amazing show of strength. I felt the numbers were far greater than the two hundred and fifty thousand mentioned on the news that night.

Anyway, in a quiet moment I decided to work out the height of the London pigeons I'd been watching flying round the multi-storey tower blocks. Assuming an average of 10 feet per floor, a pigeon flying at 12th floor level was a 40-yarder and the 15th floor bird a 50-yarder. In practice pigeons flying at that height looked so small one would not have raised one's gun to them.

I checked my calculations with Nelson's Column as we marched past. Our great nautical hero stood 157 feet above our army of committed countrymen that Sunday morning. He looked proud of us – yes, very proud of us, but I know the pigeons flying round his feet would have been very safe as few shots would have considered them remotely shootable except for the few world champions like George Digweed and Richard Faulds.

We pigeon shooters are good at judging range of birds over decoys or low crossing shots. They are much easier to judge when related to the ground and horizon. Also a 40-yard crosser looks perfectly shootable because like the moon on the horizon, it looks big but the same bird 40 yards up is subject to the opposite optical illusion and appears very much smaller.

With that thought for the day I'll move on!

Pigeon Migration

Do pigeons migrate? This is a much debated and little researched question over which there is great controversy. I believe the answer is some do and many do not. There is always a resident population in an area, the density of which will depend on the balance of feed, roosting and nesting habitat throughout the year.

At the end of the summer there will be flocks of young birds which will need to move on to find adequate winter food whether this be rape or southern England's woodland harvest of acorns and beechmast. Conversely, in the spring there is a movement north following the spring drilling which starts in the south in late January and can go on until late May in parts of Scotland. It is not a global migration that takes place but in Britain a national movement mainly of birds of the year.

With the advent of winter rape since the 1970s, and in more recent times it being grown further and further north in Scotland, it is probable that fewer pigeons need to move south in winter. The northern resident population is now much greater than it was in the past, when winters were harder and a meagre living on turnip tops was all that was available.

A few years ago I was migrating north myself in the third week of May to work on painting commissions on the rivers of Sutherland where few woodpigeon ever venture in summer, let alone winter. I had been invited to visit a mutual pigeon fanatic in Aberdeenshire, Andy Hill. We first met on the BASC woodpigeon working group on which he represented Scotland. Our rendezvous on this occasion was at his handsome stone-built house up in the hills above Deeside. We would cover some interesting and very beautiful pigeon country in Andy's Land Rover. Wide open valleys of mixed farms with small fields gave way to hill farms and heather-topped hills and grouse moors. Some valleys were sparsely wooded but other areas were forested. The glens were rich with mature hardwoods which had only just broken into leaf.

One afternoon we visited an area where two large fields, each of about 70 acres, had been drilled with barley two weeks earlier. A haze of 2-inch green blades rose and fell across the rolling fields but the most exciting thing about it all was that there were perhaps four to five hundred pigeons spread evenly across these two fields, feeding enthusiastically.

Andy knows his area which covers about a hundred farms. With the poor April weather in the north, the pigeons had arrived late from the south. It was interesting that on the subject of pigeon movement we were in total agreement – maybe we were both wrong but we thought that we were looking at pigeons which were not in these fields a week ago. He had not fired a shot on this farm this spring. On inspecting the fields we could see that the attraction was partly undersown grass seed as well as the ungerminated barley on the surface which had not been gleaned soon after drilling – which obviously meant that there were no pigeons there earlier.

So next day we arrived at 10.30 a.m. to look again and, sure enough, even at that time there was activity with odd pigeons and small groups arriving from two main lines. It looked good but Andy was apprehensive that it might dry up by midday.

We decided to set up and see, and to shoot from two hides almost on the diagonal corners of the large square area. We would both have a crosswind as it turned out, as the wind backed to improve for both of us as the day progressed.

I was soon in action and it was fast and furious. In fact by the time Andy was set up an hour later I'd shot fifty. The pigeons worked in a big circle when he started shooting and the day became fairly even for us both. The day brightened into the most ideal conditions, clear sky with broken cloud, sometimes a brief shower and all with a fresh westerly wind. I could see Andy's decoys with the naked eye even though we were about three-quarters of a mile apart. The light was very clear and the pigeons showed up well on the soft green crop. Certainly the pigeons could see the decoys, as at times groups came in at great height over the grouse moors to Andy's left and just folded their wings. At other times he said they came like snipe through the whins below the heather line. This was because a peregrine was playing and doing feint stoops on these passing pigeons and making them very skittish.

I had shot at a crow early in the day and set it up to the right of my decoy pattern. Another came and I did likewise. I ended up shooting twenty-four carrions and two hoodies by the end of the day, which was a record for me. The secret was that I was in a very good hide on the edge of a black conifer strip and in shade when the sun was out.

Andy pointed out that the farming was similar to how farming in England was in the 1960s but with the addition of a few fields of winter rape. As was suggested earlier this is the reason for more resident winter pigeon in Scotland.

I found I had much in common with Andy in terms of approach, belief and techniques of decoying although he did surprise me with his maxim of the three Ss for pigeon. The first two are probably self-explanatory – Seed and Safety – but Andy feels that the flock offers the same opportunities for wild times like clubbing and pubbing, hence Sex! His pigeon north of the border do seem oversexed according to his stories of pigeon trying to mount his decoys and floaters, or gang-raping a bird on the ground. My Cambridgeshire southern pigeon lead a very sober and puritanical life compared with the rape and pillage in the North!

Average days for his clients produce bags of thirty to forty birds so our day of 393 head, including crows, was exceptional. But, Andy pointed out, as we had only fired 508 shots between us, our score rate was high. On our return Andy's cheerful partner Kitty greeted us, late though we were, with a marvellous meal. As we collapsed into armchairs afterwards with glass in hand, we had to agree that these pigeons had migrated from the south!

Argentinian Adventure

Jet-lagged and deprived of sleep, it was pure adrenaline that kept me going for three and a half days of the most sensational shooting possible.

The doves of Argentina are a plague to farmers, at times decimating crops and preventing some, such as sunflowers, being grown at all. These are the eared dove, about half the size of our collared dove and more the size of a starling. They make a woodpigeon look like a jumbo jet and have the characteristics of a spitfire. I anticipated numbers but I did not expect them to fly so high and fast over the flat ground of the area we were shooting. These doves must be the ultimate shotgun sporting challenge.

This exciting trip all came about when Barry Littlewood, an English friend who lives and runs a very successful business in New Jersey, was talking to me about doing a painting commission for him. Barry is one of those people with endless energy for life. This includes a fanatical passion for shooting and a hyperactive trigger finger to match. If he's not actually shooting something then he's thinking about it. Little surprise that we became friends. He was keen to investigate dove shooting in Argentina and suggested I join him and three chums of his when I was over to do the painting. In mid-June the dream came true.

I had flown to Newark, the airport south of New York, and stayed overnight at Barry's home where we all met up. Roger Whiffen is the manager of Barry's farm and sporting estate nearby. A true East Anglian, an English oak of a man who was in his late 40s, he gave up managing a most efficient and productive farm near Newmarket and moved with his wife Liz and son Simon to take on this new challenge. Billy Daniels, in his early 30s, is a lawyer from Carolina who had recently come north to work for Barry's company. He's another who lives for 'hunting', a word that encompasses all shooting, stalking and fishing activities in the USA. Finally Mike Parks, again from the Deep South on the North Carolina coast where fishing and boat-building are his business, and duck shooting his passion. A short, stocky guy who wears his baseball cap twenty-four hours a day, he is a gun fanatic and has a great sense of deep southern humour.

We arrived in Buenos Aires to find our internal flight had been postponed for eight hours. The good news was that repairs to the plane had been completed. The bad news was that an arsonist had set fire to the control tower the day before so few flights could arrive or depart. Doubt and scepticism set in.

By now we had met up with the rest of the party, who included Bob and Frances, a charming couple in their early 70s from Florida, Bob from Boston and Roger, two middle-aged Americans who lived for partying twenty-four hours a day.

With increasing doubt as to whether our plane would actually fly at all, Roger suggested we charter a plane. 'It's only money', he said. I gulped but we had to agree it was the best idea. Sylvia, our efficient courier lady, was soon overheating her mobile phone to make it happen – and we were airborne in a 12-seater within an hour.

The luxury lodge in Cordoba where we were to be accommodated was in an area flooded out by El Niño, the torrential rains and freak weather to hit South America that year. The duck hides we were to have shot from one day were twelve feet under water. The doves had moved because all the fields where they feed were under water also.

Trek International, the company we were with, had to move us further north to a new area they are opening up. We therefore flew to Tucuman, the largest town in the area, and stayed at the Grand Hotel. This had all the indistinguishable characteristics of international hotels, and was comfortable but impersonal. However, the steaks were exceptionally good for dinner.

We got a 5.30 a.m. call next morning and after an early breakfast we left the hotel in a ten-seater van. We drove south-east for an hour and as the sun rose we arrived on a vast, flat, arable plain with some large areas of scrub. We were dropped off along a dirt track about 60 yards apart at points where a bird boy was standing beside two 250-cases of cartridges. I was on the far end of the line and doves, high in the dawn sky, were already passing overhead.

For various reasons I had not brought my own guns and for various other reasons the side-by-side I was to borrow from Barry met with paperwork problems at the New York Argentinean Embassy. So I borrowed a Beretta over-under from Trek and a 20 bore pump action from Mike Parks.

Being a traditional side-by-side shot I was soon in trouble. I fired a box of cartridges without a feather to show for it. Was it me, the high, fast doves, the cartridges or the gun? All I knew was that I could not get the picture right. Halfway through the second box I tried something I had done in desperation before when using a weapon so different from my own, which was to close my left eye. Not a good habit and anathema to all I do normally to shoot spontaneously. However, this rifling technique did improve things dramatically and soon these tiny little birds were being plucked out of the sky at what seemed ridiculously long range.

We were using Fiocchi cartridges which are made in Argentina. They were 28 gm No 8 or 7½ shot and as I got used to them I believe they were very fast. Their high pressure meant I was glad of the shoulder recoil pad in which I had invested before leaving home.

The morning had been hectic, shooting for an hour or so and then easing to a steady trickle and gunfire the full length of the line. As the sun rose I hid in the shadow of a large cactus. These grew here and there amongst the scrub thorns to about 12 feet high and were the type with big ears covered in spines. I was relieved to hear that others in the party, using their own guns, had trouble at first hitting the doves. However, things had improved and we'd all shot over a case of cartridges.

The early morning was chilly but by midday it was like a really fine day in May or September. We enjoyed a lazy lunch with the most succulent steak barbecued beside the derelict farm building. Farm equipment around the yard of this 8,000 acre estate was basic: combine harvesters of 1950s and 60s design with external driving belts which would have made a health and safety inspector choke and splutter before closing the place down.

At 3.30 p.m. we were driven a short distance and then dropped off on another dirt road beside our two cases of cartridges. I had not had a bird boy in the morning but in the afternoon I was met by Abdo, a cheerful, enthusiastic lad in his mid-teens. A few words of Spanish surfaced from my trips to Spain partridge shooting in the 1970s but sadly communication was limited. However, thumbs up or down seemed universal and the counter was clicked on the successful thumbs up as another dove spun from the sky like a sycamore seed.

The flight started slowly but from about five o'clock, for an hour I'd never seen anything like it. As fast as one could load, there were more birds in the air, jinking, darting or just flighting over. They came singly, in scattered groups or flocks like starlings. The main line for me was over my right shoulder and at about 30 yards high. Still mostly with my left eye shut, I was thrilled to account for 277 for the 527 shots I'd fired. Some evening flight!

Next day we had an incredible half hour at dawn. Doves just poured over, again at the 30 yard range going out to feed. I've never shot a hundred birds as fast. We then moved to where doves were flighting between feed areas. Bob was already in position 30–40 yards away and after I'd shot for a while I went to see how he was getting on with his superb pair of side-by-side Piotti guns. He then told me he had first gone to my position and after a few shots heard a rattling in the bush beside him. His boy pointed to a rattlesnake just 4 feet from him. Bob fired both barrels at point blank range, killing the snake. Not surprisingly then, he had felt unhappy in that position, so moved. I had then come along and been put in the place – with the dead rattlesnake hidden under the bush. I later heard they usually live in pairs. I'm glad that chap was on his own!

The afternoon surprised me as we went back to the same roost as the day before. I was in a different position and saw even more doves. I was now running out of superlatives as each day and flight seemed the more exciting. I had started to use the 20 bore pump action also with my one-eyed-bandit technique. I kept forgetting to pump the action but it did mount so fast and easily I soon got it going well. It was the biggest shoot of my lifetime with 420 doves for 643 shots – at least the practice is improving my average even if it is ruining my shooting technique.

The following day we shot morning and afternoon on an enormous area of soya stubble with doves either coming to feed or visiting the waterhole at the ranch nearby. By now we were all on such a high. I could hear Barry's voice getting higher and higher as yet another stratospheric dove succumbed to his Bonelli 12 bore automatic. From another quarter I could hear a deep Southern drawl as a 'Yeerp' expressed Billy's exhilaration when his heavy Beretta 'onyx' spiralled a long shot.

After three and a half days, Junior and Gestave, who had organised everything so well, and scouted and worked so hard for us with all their back-up team, said farewell as we checked in our baggage to fly back to Buenos Aires. At our final lunch he had given our cartridge account. The five in our party had fired a total of 17,200 shots, Barry's hyperactive trigger finger alone had twitched 4000 times.

An amazing shooting experience, yes indeed, but I return home with an even greater love and respect for our own woody.

Why was it not a Chicken that Crossed the Road?

When is a woodpigeon not a woodpigeon? When it's 'chicken', 'seagull', 'albino' or a 'grouse'. Puzzled? Yes, so have I been during the past month by these four descriptions of the handsome grey bird with striking white neck ring and wing bars that we all agree is a woodpigeon.

However, my 14-year-old niece told me a story about a pigeon which flew into the side of the school bus and as it bounced off, a cloud of pale grey feathers exploded from the bird. Whether dead or alive history does not relate but most of the children thought it was a 'chicken'. These were not inner city children but children from a small country town or the nearby villages. Why, I asked, did they think it was a chicken: ignorance of the countryside multiplied tenfold by her answer – 'Because it had feathers.' Do not all birds have feathers, I pondered? My niece put them right, I'm glad to report.

It makes me despair at the prospect of the countryside, let alone country sports or the future of world ecology which will one day be in the hands of their generation. Our generation is at fault for not teaching them the basic facts for the survival of our species – clean air, water and fertile soil. After these vital elements have been destroyed people cannot eat PCs, TVs or compact discs.

As for a 'seagull'. Yes, this was the title of a picture of a carved wooden decoy woodpigeon from early last century in an elegant coffee table book on interior design with glossy pages and high price: surely the printed word must be right? Oh dear, maybe the author went to the same school as my niece.

The 'albino' is fact, as the photograph proved which was sent to me by a pigeon shooter. Albino woodpigeons are unusual but not rare and one does see them from time to time. Actually in my area of East Anglia we try not to shoot them as they are interesting marker birds in a flock. Some time ago I had one in the garden – it arrived in the spring and stayed for two or three months before disappearing. I feared it had been shot but it came back the next year and for two years after that, again arriving in the spring and leaving in mid-summer. I therefore knew it was a minimum of four years old but preferred to go and nest elsewhere as it never stayed and nested in my garden. I have seen albino specimens, stuffed, in collections from the Victorian and Edwardian eras. Sadly, albino white feathers turn a dusty light brown with age and eventually do not do justice to the beauty achieved by the taxidermist at the time.

Finally the pigeon as a 'grouse' was my experience one day in late September. I had been watching a 25-acre bean stubble with interest while a good number of pigeons were building up on it. The day I chose to shoot was very windy, much too windy in normal circumstances to make a good bag. However, an amazingly sporting day developed. The field was rectangular with one long side next to a road. The opposite side had a ditch and a good hedge with mature ash trees and was an ideal site for a hide with the wind along the hedge from my left. This generated the steady shooting of pigeons coming on the flight line from my right. It worked well for an hour or so with an easy first shot of pigeon battling into the wind but a fiendishly difficult second shot as any other birds flared away downwind at the sound of the first shot. Nevertheless it was fast and furious sport for a while.

As the day continued the wind changed and began quartering into me, which was far from ideal. However, this meant that any pigeons out over the field on the side near the road were disturbed and flew downwind straight over me. The wind was so strong by now that they flew low across the bean stubble and presented shots as exciting as those on any grouse drive.

As my hide was in the dry ditch in front of the hedge, my eye level was not much higher than the field, which helped to enhance the illusion of the view from a grouse butt. I could just imagine the pigeons as singles or coveys of grouse skimming at me low across the heather on a downwind drive – a dream drive that went on for three or four hours! It was a big day with continuous sport as the pigeon came at me disorientated by such a high wind. I ended up with just over two hundred, or one hundred brace in grouse terms! I dare not equate the economics with the cost of driven grouse at £150 per brace.

MOVE, MOUNT, SHOOT WITH JOHN BIDWELL

Loving all forms of shooting as I do, I am always very interested in shooting techniques. There are certain considerations that are imperative and all coaches and good shots will agree that unless the gun fits and is mounted consistently, an individual cannot shoot accurately. In other words the gun, when mounted, must be an extension of the right eye for a normal right-handed, right master-eyed shot. That sounds simple but there are many problems of footwork or gunmounting which can prevent this from being achieved. I am not a trained coach and suggest you visit a good instructor if you have a problem.

Where you place the shot, or to be more correct, where you think you should place the shot, is quite another matter. I look carefully at the potential target whether game, pigeon or clay and shoot quite fast. While I'm focused on the bird, my gun is slowly moving in relation to the target and always ahead of it: if I had to describe my own technique I would say it was a 'think ahead' method. I believe what I do is to look at the target but my peripheral vision is moving my gun to point ahead, which feels right. Why it is right I don't know but with experience I just sense it is.

In September one year I visited John Bidwell at his shooting ground in Suffolk. John is not only a world champion shot in a number of clay disciplines but a remarkable coach. His move, mount, shoot method he uses so effectively and teaches so positively is a natural and instinctive technique. It relies on our inborn ability to judge speed, line and distance. If a ball is thrown, we just put a hand out to catch it. Our hand moves by natural reaction to the correct position to catch the ball. We do not come from behind, point and pull through or calculate a maintained lead. We just move, mount and catch.

This is close to what I do when shooting well. However, as soon as we begin not shooting well we let our minds take over and start calculating, believing that our conscious mind must be superior to our subconscious reaction. What happens - we shoot worse, not better.

I find John's method is particularly effective on crossers at any speed, height or angle. Try it sometime - focus on the target, hold the gun low and ahead of the bird and slowly move with it. Mount smoothly and whilst still focusing on the target let the gun point where it wants and fire at the 'feel right' moment. If it works then visit John Bidwell who will show you more. If it does not work then go and see John who will explain it much better than I have in these few words.*

*For more information either read John Bidwell's book, *Move, Mount, Shoot* published by Crowood Press or visit High Lodge Shooting School, near Saxmundham, Suffolk for a lesson or group clinic, tel. 01986 784347.

Cammo Kit

Cammo is the kit I'd never be seen dead in – but there again, neither am I seen in it alive! It is the time of year when pigeon roost shooting, that camouflage clothing can be of great help. I resisted the idea until the last year or two because, as a traditional sort of chap, I feel countrymen in cammo wear look either threateningly military or naff. However, as an ever-enthusiastic pigeon shot, I enjoy trying new ideas and experimenting.

When roost shooting there are two ways in which a sharp-eyed pigeon flying over the treetops can see us. They then immediately jink away, making the most impossible shot which one knows is a miss before the lead is halfway down the barrel. Firstly, any movement immediately betrays the presence of the roost shooter and secondly, the pale winter face, even with a hat, is so visible when looking upwards at oncoming birds. The problem of movement is still going to be obvious even if wearing the best camouflage and only experience will teach one the technique needed to remain absolutely still once pigeon are seen approaching. The way which works for me is to move my feet into the position for the anticipated shot when I see the angle of oncoming birds. At the same time, I raise my gun but not into my shoulder. The heel of the stock is at chest height. I then freeze absolutely still while the pigeons continue to approach the point at which I can take a shot, hopefully through a gap in the trees.

When that moment comes, my gun is finally mounted to my shoulder and the shot fired. Ninety per cent of the movement in preparation for the shot is therefore done before the pigeon is anywhere near.

This leaves the second vulnerable problem of one's face. Thinking from the pigeon's point of view, it is approaching looking down for other pigeons in the treetops, or for danger. So as you see him appear over a gap in the trees, he can see your face looking up. A pigeon's reactions are faster than a man's and he depends on them for his survival. That is why the challenge of pigeon shooting is so exciting.

Face masks of various types have been available for years and I do believe that for roost shooting they can be of particular benefit.

So what form of camouflage is best? The object of the exercise is to break up our outline by using shapes of colour and tone to merge with the background. As an artist I am very interested in how this works and feel that tone – the range from light to dark – is the most important. However, we do not know if the eyes of a woodpigeon see in the same range of colours and tones as those of a human.

I have recently conducted some experiments with different shooting jackets. The four I used were Realtree Xtra Brown, British Army, typical shooting tweed and a dull Gor-tex type. I hung the four on coathangers from bushes on the edge of woodland. I then photographed them at different ranges from 10 to 20 yards (I still find it difficult to say metres!). Colour and tone merged well with the background in all four cases but it was clear that the two camouflaged pattern coats optically merged best with the broken appearance of the winter bushes, trees, bramble and ivy in the woodland.

I then tried another situation in which I set the camera at 10 yards from a position where I stood in woodland wearing the different jackets. In the case of the Realtree kit, I wore not only the jacket but also trousers, gloves and head mask. The other three jackets were photographed with me wearing dull brown corduroy trousers and a cap. The Realtree Xtra Brown range was remarkable. To all intents and purposes I was invisible and it was only the gun which showed up at all. To a pigeon overhead, even this would not have been seen, as the angle of vision would be along the gun from the ends of the barrels, by which time it should have been a puff of feathers in the centre of a pattern of No 6 shot! The three other jackets were sufficiently good colour and tone in the woodland background but my face and hands were certainly very visible.

To remain still and shoot with a minimum of movement is the most important advice for all woodpigeon shooting but I do believe cammo clothing does definitely help. So maybe 'the kit I wouldn't be seen dead in' would be a brilliant advertising slogan for Realtree – one thing for sure is that it would be unique, as no other clothing manufacturer in the high street would want to use it!

Today's Menu

'What's on the menu today?' I would ask myself this if I were a woodpigeon as I awoke, fluffed my feathers and stretched my wings before settling back down on the branch to assess the weather conditions.

'I gleaned a crop full of delicious spring drilled barley yesterday but the modern drills are so mean to us pigeons that most of the tasty plump grains of seed are buried. My mates and I did not leave much by the time we lifted off the field and flew home as a flock to our roosting wood last night.

'Besides which, the overnight rain will mean my feet will ball up with mud as I potter about the newly worked soil. If it dries up I will go and have a look this afternoon. For breakfast, I will pop down to the meadow by the river where the clover is young and tasty.

'Most of my chums have gone off in a big flock to the winter rape. I can always go there later but I've got rather bored with rape for breakfast, lunch and tea throughout the winter. Mind you, it is filling and reasonably nutritious and keeps most of our present generation not just alive through the winter, but in good condition. In the old days before the advent of winter rape in the 1970s, so many of my forebears died in hard winters. In years like 1963, whole generations of us woodpigeons were lost.

'If the barley is finished then I will go and enjoy a late afternoon cropful of ivy berries. Those old trees by the church are covered with ivy and berries are available on any day, in any weather and are quite tasty and nutritious.'

So might be the thoughts of a pigeon and few birds eat such a varied diet throughout the year. This is one of the reasons for the great success of the species and why their survival rate is high. Nature is very clever, and evolution has adapted each species of bird to lay the number of eggs needed to ensure sufficient recruitment to the population without producing a population explosion, which could cause starvation through inadequate food resources. After all, if any pair of birds rear on average more than two surviving progeny in their lifetime, the population would escalate enormously. Equally, the converse is true that if, in the lifetime of a bird, one of its young does not survive then there is a population crash. This indicates the scale of losses in prolific species like blue tits, which will lay large clutches of eggs to maintain the population. Hence the importance of vermin control by a gamekeeper to enable game birds to rear a shootable surplus as well as to maintain or increase the stock of wild game on a shoot.

So pigeons, laying only two eggs in clutches over a prolonged period of the year, optimise on the wide variety of food sources available. This compares with many other species, such as tits, warblers and game birds which must feed their young on insects. They nest in the spring to make the most of the insects available in early summer.

On looking through my game books it is amazing, therefore, how many food sources have produced venues for decoying opportunities. In the spring one thinks immediately of drilled corn but, as the beginning of this article shows, a pigeon's choice is considerable from day to day. It is interesting to go through the seasons and relate them to my pigeon shooting which has been mainly in East Anglia.

Oilseed rape remains a staple diet until late spring and early summer, but linseed at the 'cress' stage, young peas, clover and lucerne are crops where shooting is necessary for crop protection.

Other tasty meals for woodpigeon in spring are of no threat to the farmer but can produce good sport. These include various weed species such as chickweed, speedwell and buttercup leaves. A problem in the spring arises when pigeons go 'budding' and spend all day in the woods eating beech or ash buds just as they break into leaf. At that time of year pigeon shooting can be frustrating as no pigeon needs to flight out to feed. It just flutters from twig to twig enjoying its most natural food and hence its appropriate name, the 'wood' pigeon.

As spring gives way to summer, peas are a favourite at any stage of the crop. Grass seed, strawberries and weeds in set-aside can all produce concentrations of feeding pigeons. In hot weather they love young mustard leaves in fields where it is grown for seed, as well as spring rape or kale game strips. Pigeons must have water and occasionally a shoot can be found based on a pond or even a water trough where pigeons regularly drink.

Laid corn is a traditional venue for summer pigeon sport but growth regulators have reduced the incidence of crops going down. However, if there is a laid patch, pigeons and rooks will find it and can do a lot of damage.

Late summer and autumn are now producing the cream of pigeon shooting, starting with rape stubbles in July and August, then barley stubble followed by wheat and finally, best of all, bean stubbles. All are subject to the timing of ploughing and the farmer's enthusiasm to plough straight behind the combine is at times frustrating. Just as the birds have found a bounteous field of shed grain, it disappears beneath the ploughshare.

In winter the pigeon is again an opportunist. In good years for acorns or beechmast, every oak and beech will be visited as they are in the spring when 'budding' – the woodpigeon lives up to its name. However, throughout the long winter months, oilseed rape will be the staple food for most pigeons. It is grown extensively throughout Britain and is the survival diet for the country's woodpigeon population.

Sugar beet tops, frosted potatoes, Brussels sprouts, turnip tops, hawthorn and ivy berries all feature as food where available. Judging by the crop contents of pigeons shot, I believe that ivy berries are becoming more and more a winter food for pigeons. They are available regularly every year, in any weather and it is for this reason that even in the rare periods of heavy snow, pigeons can survive very happily on these berries snug under the evergreen leaves shrouding the trunks of so many trees in the countryside.

Few birds have adapted to such a wide variety of food. No wonder the woodpigeon doesn't just survive, it thrives.

Roe Stalking Magic Moment

In early May I went roe stalking in Berkshire. Actually, to watch and experience the sport for an evening and dawn sortie with Trevor Hughes. He was part of the farming team on an estate with mature oak woods and pretty farms set in rolling hills. A timeless English landscape offered the perfect setting in which to accompany Trevor during our evening stalk. We tiptoed silently from glade to ride through one of the large mixed woods. There were does feeding on the far side of an area of recently planted woodland. Slots of both roe and muntjac showed clearly in the soft mud in depressions on the route we took. As I have really very little experience of stalking roe, Trevor quietly talked me through the sights and sounds, and told stories of successful stalks in the past or the frustrations of an elusive buck.

We eventually settled to wait on a cross ride. We sat on the soft, young grass, our backs against a tree in silence, our senses honed for sight or sound. There were many of both. For the last hour of that Saturday evening in the peace and tranquillity of that wood the world was a perfect place. The view down the ride ahead was a natural composition for a painting. A birch leaned from the left framing the dappled young greens which were broken by bands of bluebells. There were tits in the oak above us and a tree creeper spiralling in and out of sight in the trunk of an ash. Then the hairs on our necks stiffened as they did on the back of Corrie, Trevor's German wire-haired pointer. Silently an elegant roe appeared 60 yards ahead and then another. Both were does so we relaxed again to watch through our binoculars. A greater spotted woodpecker flew across a gap in the trees, then a woodcock, not roding but obviously a resident breeding bird. Trevor told me how the woodsman had seen one carrying young between its legs, flying awkwardly across that same ride a few summers ago. A pipistrelle bat zoomed about as dusk fell, flying like a kite out of control, down, across, twisting upwards again. Throughout, Trevor's passion for roe stalking was evident in his interpretation of each of nature's clues.

My pigeon shooter's eye could not help reading their story either. Some flew past as displaying pairs, others returned high to roost having perhaps fed on young peas or having nipped off tender beech buds for their supper. A full, exciting evening had been enjoyed by the two of us in our different ways on that same stage set by mother nature. Not a chance of a shot but we agreed the magic of the evening was complete without a deer.

Where and when do we find and consequently develop these deep feelings, this devotion to the countryside? I suspect for most of us it is in early childhood experiences with parents, grandparents or the adults around us. I know for me it was the walk across the meadows behind our house with my father. He was no Conrad Lawrence, no biologist, just a loving father who enjoyed time shared walking together. We marvelled at chance sightings of stoat, barn owl or peewit. He did not fish or shoot much but occasionally we'd go fishing for roach and minnows in the river nearby or I would hide under a hedge as he flighted a few pigeon home to their evening roost. What worries me about the future of the countryside, let alone country sports, is how few children are fortunate enough to enjoy these early experiences.

However, I am encouraged to see that I am not alone in my thinking, and that The Countryside Foundation for Education has been formed to address this vacuum in so many children's lives. It is an initiative sponsored by a number of industries, individuals and charitable trusts. Maybe we can all help. I was involved in running two trial courses one summer on my little shoot and reserve for primary and secondary school teachers. This was an opportunity to enthuse children through their teachers and to link country facts to country feelings. Of course, I pointed out a woodpigeon when one flew over!

Aberdeenshire Bonus

Some years ago I formed a friendship with Andy Hill, when he was the Scottish representative on the BASC Woodpigeon Working Group. A year later Andy kindly invited me to join him in Aberdeenshire on the way back from one of my river painting commission trips in the Highlands. We were kindred spirits in the way we saw and assessed pigeons in the area: whilst sometimes wrong, we certainly got it right on that particular occasion and were rewarded with some exciting sport.

I travelled from Strath Naver where I'd painted for a week in Sutherland. I had seen a few pigeons on drilling on my way through Perthshire but as I wound my way south that evening it was not until 10 miles from my destination that I spotted a very promising field. On my arrival Andy casually enquired as to whether I'd seen any pigeons, so I told him. Amused, he wryly said: 'Trust Garfit to find the only hot field in the area.' It was actually the field to be shot the next day.

The following morning brought promising signs with a good number of pigeons feeding on the drilled spring wheat by 10 a.m. It was surprising to see so many that early as the main feeding time was not expected until mid-afternoon.

Frank, a friend of Andy's, was set up on the main flight line from some forestry a mile west of the field. Many of the field boundaries in the area were wire stock fences with few natural hedges for hides. Andy had the construction of a hide against a wire fence down to a fine art with adjustable poles and hazel sticks taped together to form a skeletal structure on which to hang nets and spruce branches as a background and partial roof. Decoys were set out and Frank was shooting before we had even arrived at the second position where I was to set up 400 yards away on the fence at right angles to the first hide. I was soon also in business and in half an hour had developed a full pattern of dead birds as decoys which worked like a charm. Sport for both of us was fast and furious from about 11 a.m. until 1 p.m.

The mist began to thicken causing more birds to come to me, and I could hear fewer shots from Frank. Andy had us all linked by mobile radios, so I suggested swapping with Frank, but Andy said to continue for a while longer. By 2 p.m. I had shot a hundred and insisted that we must swap over. We did and Frank continued to have a great shoot all afternoon. Not that it was completely quiet at Frank's original hide!

I tried to get Andy to take over and have some sport but he was too conscientious to shoot and enjoyed keeping Frank well looked after. Andy's quad bike was a saviour at the end of a session when well over two hundred pigeon were accounted for. It was a day of pigeon decoying at its best whether in Scotland or for that matter anywhere in the British Isles.

Prior to retiring to France, Andy and Kitty welcomed me to stay on a number of occasions. Kitty is a wonderful cook and hostess but finds Andy and me a hopeless pair as we find it difficult to divert from our favourite topic of conversation – pigeons!

PAINTER'S PERKS

The eyes and ears of a pigeon shooter are never switched off. It is not just when actually out on reconnaissance looking for a shootable situation that our senses are tuned to our favourite sporting quarry. We notice pigeons flighting across the road whether we are driving to work, on holiday or just popping down to the garage. Those specks on the horizon, invisible to or unnoticed by the drivers of a hundred cars in front and behind, are instantly recognised by us as woodpigeon. We feel a tingle of adrenaline as we sight those sporting birds.

While I sit for hours painting commissions on rivers from the south coast of England to the north coast of Scotland, I cannot help seeing or hearing any pigeons that move or coo. Occasionally I see an irresistible line of birds crossing my view. This happened a few years ago when painting the Tweed. When I stopped for a sandwich I decided to follow the line and find out where those pigeons were feeding. Not far away I discovered a stubble field shimmering with a blue haze of pigeon. I watched for a while and observed that the flight line coming past my painting view was only one of three to the field. I watched again the following day and though fewer birds were there it was still a very hot field. Later on I found the owner and got permission to go shooting the next day.

It was not a big field and I knew that the number of pigeons would soon glean that stubble bare. I borrowed a gun and cartridges from my cousin with whom I was staying. I shot a few birds coming high over a hedge to start a decoy pattern and then went on to shoot just over one hundred from only a third of the number I had seen feeding on my first sighting two days earlier. I thanked the owner and gave the pigeons to the keeper to sell and get a drink out of what had been a bonus day's sport for me. Sadly, my painting trips do not often produce such sporting diversions.

Oxford v. Cambridge

Even had I been to university rather than art school I would never have been one of those intelligent young things on University Challenge. However, I did experience a pigeon shooter's equivalent on two consecutive days' shooting at the end of July one year.

Cambridge is my home patch and I had been watching a good line of pigeons coming out of the town for two or three days to feed on rape stubble. Town suburbs provide the most perfect habitat for pigeons with an intensive patchwork of gardens, all with trees, hedges and shrubs in which pigeons set up home; clover and weeds in the lawns, fresh salads in the vegetable gardens and an easy flight for a main meal at an out of town venue on the surrounding farms.

The situation on a series of adjoining fields south of Cambridge was interesting as the first rape fields harvested had been disced to chiddle the top inch or two in order to stimulate germination of the split seed. (This helps clean the ground for subsequent winter drilled wheat.) The pigeons were still feeding on these rape stubbles and the main line passed a certain bush on one of the hedges.

The day I could shoot was a Wednesday and I set out at midday intending to go straight to the hedgerow my reconnaissance had indicated as the optimum spot. However, there was a large 70-acre field of winter rape a few fields away which had been combined over the past two or three days and there was another good line going out to this new rape stubble. This field was not on a farm on which I had permission to shoot but I felt I might find a spot where I could intercept the two flight lines before the pigeons went over the boundary. If it worked there would be a big shoot and I usually like to go for a risky challenge. However, my bluff was called. I tried two positions, both worked only moderately, the problem being that the pigeons on the first main line I had spotted all landed short on the original disced rape stubble.

So, at 3 p.m. I decided to cut my losses and accept the failure of plan B and revert to my initial idea of catching the one good line. This did work as intended and produced good decoying shots as well as the bonus of some downwind driven birds returning from the other distant rape stubbles. By 7 p.m. activity had declined and it was time to pack up. In hindsight I should have gone with my first plan which would have given another good three hours' shooting but these intelligent Cambridge pigeons beat me. However, I ended with a bag of 103.

The following day Phil Beasley had invited me to come out for a day. He had two clients that day and we were soon on a farm north of Oxford where they were set up on promising rape stubbles. Then William, Phil's son, and David, another member of the team, took me to a big field of wheat where there were some open, laid patches. The farmer had telephoned two days earlier to say how much damage the pigeons were doing.

It was a great treat to have help from Will and David to carry my kit along the 5–600 yards of tramlines across the near field of standing wheat to get to the hedgerow to shoot the further field favoured by the pigeons. I'm not so good at travelling light and normally set off loaded like a packhorse, but on this occasion I felt positively pampered.

It was not long before I was in action. The pigeon magnet was particularly useful and effective at drawing birds from the main laid patch in the middle of the field to the smaller patches nearer my hide in the hedge.

I had started at about 1.30 p.m. and by 5 p.m., when David came to visit me again, I had already shot eighty. This was exciting enough but little did I realise what was to come. The weather had been dull and overcast but had kept dry. However, at between 6 and 6.30 p.m. the sky cleared to produce a most beautiful summer evening. The breeze kept up from the south-west and the woodpigeons from Oxford obviously decided it was a good evening for a meal out of town. They came steadily in groups and small parties right across the field to me, producing fantastic shooting for three hours. They were still coming at 8 p.m. but I realised how difficult picking up was going to be for Conon, my four-year-old golden retriever. So I stopped at 8.15 by which time I could hardly believe there were another 190 on my clicker: a total of 270 for the day. I picked up everything on the laid patches before carefully working Conon in the standing wheat. By that time David had come to help and, with a loaded rucksack on his back and bag over his shoulder, carried off 120 pigeons on the first trip. It would have killed me but he was obviously not just young but very strong and fit. With intervals for water from the bottle I had taken for him, Conon worked amazingly well and whilst one will never pick all the birds in a standing crop, we got most of them.

On my way home that night, after a good supper back at Phil's house, I contemplated two exceptional and interesting days – one with Cambridge pigeons and the other with those from Oxford. So the pigeon shooter's University Challenge concluded that whilst those from Oxford were more numerous and sporting, those from Cambridge were cleverer. Whoops – what a provocative and dangerous statement to publish. I hope nobody from either university will take that personally. However, as I am sure no academic from Cambridge or Oxford would be reading this anyway, I have nothing to fear.

Reciprocal Pigeon Days
with Peter Theobald

The Game Fair is a great meeting place for thousands of us with a common gene; that of the hunter-gatherer. That gene is as strong today as it was in our Neolithic forbears. It is a gene that has enabled man not just to survive but to thrive. It would have been those early hunter-gatherers who knew, understood and respected their quarry and the habitat in which it lived. It was a small jump in evolution for man to develop his hunting skills and acknowledge the thrill derived from the pursuit of game to the point in history where it became sport.

Of all the sporting folk and friends at the Game Fair a few years ago I was interested to meet Peter Theobald with his wife, Francis. We had met briefly at a BASC roadshow the previous year but this time we had more time to chat about our passion for pigeon shooting. Peter, like me, is of the 'loner' breed of pigeon shooter. We do a lot of reconnaissance and then pounce when the day, the wind and weather seem right. We parted with a plan to share a day together if a suitable situation should arise when two loners may be better than one.

I had very much enjoyed reading Peter's book *The Woodpigeon the Ultimate Quarry*, published in 1996. It is very good and came from the heart of a dedicated pigeon shooter. His name is well known in the clay pigeon world as he won the British Skeet Championship in 1986. So he is a brilliant shot and amused me with his story of the 1991 championship which he lost to the rising star George Digweed. Having each shot one hundred straight they then went on to a marathon shoot-off in which Peter missed the 375th and George Digweed won with 375 straight! What an amazing feat by them both. What purpose, focus and concentration they have.

A fortnight after we met, Peter phoned: 'Could you come tomorrow?' A rapid rethink on my plan for the next day and, 'Yes, I'd love to.' Peter has been involved in farming in Essex all his life, a part of the world I do not know at all well. We met in a lay-by south of Chelmsford at 11 a.m. and went a few miles south to his home where Francis had the kettle on for a quick cup of coffee (and addictive oat biscuits) beside his garden duck pond. Then off further south into deepest Essex. To be honest it was becoming more and more urbanised with few farms. We passed signs to Basildon, Billericay, Rayleigh and Rochford on the left and right on our mystery tour which looked like ending on the beach at Southend. Suddenly, in the middle of Hadleigh High Street, we turned off down a crack between two shops. A dead-end sign made the prospect of shooting even less likely. However, we then went through a farm gate behind the shops and wound our way along a track and as we came round the south side of the farmhouse itself we beheld the biggest surprise of all – we were on top of a hill looking down over the enormous panorama of the Thames Estuary. Beyond lay the Isle of Sheppey to the east; all the southern shore of the estuary; the ruins of Hadleigh Castle below on the right and Canvey Island.

We stopped and looked down the hill over a large pea stubble only harvested two days earlier but with a few early feeding pigeons already dropping in on one edge. Peter suggested I shoot this field. He wanted to go to a rape stubble we could see half a mile away down below on the flood plain. He had seen pigeons on his reconnaissance the day before using both fields and going from one to another and so the plan was that by shooting both fields we would keep them moving between us.

I set up at the bottom of the hill where trees and bushes seemed to be a draw to the main line of birds coming from the north. I was soon having some very sporting shots at pigeons flying high overhead or passing along the tree tops. They were reluctant to decoy but the flight line coming to the field on a wide frontage funnelled down the hill to my position. Even though after a while I had a good number of dead birds set up as decoys, they still did not pull birds in. However, passing pigeons produced every form of exciting shot. By now I could hear Peter also having steady shooting. There was a line of pigeon passing further to my left going straight out to his rape stubble. I soon realised that if things continued we were in for a big day. I had one hundred birds by 2.30 p.m. and Peter was by then having as much, if not more, shooting. Still my pigeons would not decoy and I decided they had either not had time since the field was harvested to really feed there or that they did not feel comfortable dropping down hill against the wind into the shelter below treetop height. At 4 p.m. Peter's shots slowed down dramatically and then went silent. My shoot continued and then he appeared to see how things were going. He could not hear my shots as he had been upwind of me. He had picked 120 before his shoot had finished but then he joined me for the last hour to share my hide. Interestingly, his pigeons had decoyed perfectly on the rape stubble and he was therefore amazed to see how different things were on my field. We both egged each other on with long passing shots. An amazing day with 344 pigeons between us and a landscape background which was a joy to me, a landscape painter.

How could one repay such a day's sport, excitement, interest and beauty? Well, I knew I could not. However, a week or so later I did find an unusual situation to show Peter. A similar spontaneous phone call the night before and he was at my house next morning by 10 a.m.

I have two adjacent pea fields over which I have shot many pigeons. However, the draw is not only the peas but the large cement quarry behind. I had noticed pigeons coming for miles to then drop 200 feet to the bottom of the quarry.

I had always thought it was the water there but now, having watched carefully, I realised they come and sit on the chalk plateau base so it must be the calcium or some mineral that is important to them. Afterwards they rise to fly out of the pit and feed on the peas.

Peter and I watched for a while. I wanted him to have the best position. However, from what I had seen on the previous few days, there were two equally good spots. On this particular morning there was a very active flight line using the south-western point and at that time very little was happening on the other place which had looked good the day before. Therefore Peter went on the active line and set off on the walk to get there, travelling very light by my standards. A very fit, athletic chap in trainers, he bounced along like a young man with the bare minimum of kit on his back. He at least had an easy hedge with overgrown elders in which to make a hide and was soon in business with shots at regular intervals at wide or high birds heading for the quarry.

I watched a while and still saw little to back my observations of the previous day but decided it would be the best position to complement the line Peter was on. I was perched in a net hide nearly on the rim of the quarry top so I could get birds coming in or out; in, like normal pigeons or driven partridges; out, like driven grouse. I soon got a shot or two and then it picked up more and more as the day went on.

We were both really going well but I could see rain coming in from behind Peter. Then the clouds split and went off to the south so we had a reprieve. The same thing happened an hour later with a serious thunderstorm which went round to the west.

Sadly at about 5.30 p.m. persistent rain came and we met in the car for a cup of tea. We had been in touch every hour on my Mickey Mouse walkie-talkies which are so useful at times like that. By 6.30 p.m. we could see no light in the west and so packed up with a total of 263 pigeon between us before rain stopped play.

Our roles were reversed that day as Peter had had a testing flight line shoot with few decoying but the bulk of the pigeon traffic. I had had fewer birds but many had decoyed well over a prolonged period.

Peter had been amazed at the situation of the quarry as I had been at the surprise view of the lower Thames Estuary. We had obviously brought each other good luck to produce a joint bag of 607 from our first two away days together. It is unlikely to ever happen like that again but I shall not be far from the phone! I hope we'll share a day together again whether home or away.

Is Highest Best?

It is interesting that high driven pheasants cost more than those less vertically challenged, yet all are cheap in comparison to Britain's most expensive game bird, the grouse, which flies lowest of all. Nobody says they are unsporting!

A party of American Guns who had enjoyed pheasant shooting in the UK decided to try their hands at grouse. Their first drive produced birds skimming fast over the heather following the contours of the moor like Exocet missiles. They burst over the short skyline in front of the butts presenting the ultimate challenge. However, not a shot was fired. The keeper at the end of the drive was more puzzled than angry as he enquired why the guns had scarcely fired a shot. 'Gee, when in the UK, we've been told not to take low birds', was the reply!

However, what of the pheasant? Does it have to be high to be worthy of a sporting shot? Not necessarily, and I would guess, and bet, that more pheasants are shot in a season below 25 yards than above. A bird flying at 25 yards would be well over the average tree-top height and is a perfectly sporting pheasant.

Apart from the few fortunate shoots with ideal topography, probably 90 per cent of shoots would love their pheasants to fly higher. As Guns, we enjoy the challenge of high birds.

So what is a high pheasant? This, to my mind, is dependent on the weapon and for a traditional side-by-side shotgun with normal chokes and cartridges of 28 to 32 gm loads then 35 to 45 yards is a high and killable bird. The shot pattern and density, without getting too technical, can kill cleanly and consistently if put in the right place and that, for most of us, is the difficulty. Those with heavy over-unders with full and extra full chokes, 34 gm+ loads and the skill to use them would consider birds of 45 to maybe 60 yards as high. If a gun and cartridge could be made to kill at 100 yards then someone with exceptional skill, like world champion George Digweed and a few others, would, with a bit of practice, be able to kill birds at that range and so then even a 60-yard bird would be considered to be a low one! I know that is taking the argument over the top but it makes the point that there is no one set of figures for all people and all weapons.

So given the choice, what do we want? We want birds which can produce thrilling shooting and can be killed cleanly within our individual capabilities with a gun we enjoy using. For some this is the specialist high bird shoots of the South West where great thrill and satisfaction are derived from seeing a stratospheric bird fold and take what seems a millennium to come to earth. The ethical price to be paid is that not all are killed cleanly and one often sees a bird twitch and then plane off into the distance. Pickers-up are usually extremely effective and these wounded birds may be accounted for. However, the Gun can have several 'iffy' ones during a drive, not knowing whether a bird has been picked and therefore not having any corresponding satisfaction. In fact often a bird is struck and one has no sensation of having hit it at all. So if it is picked, perhaps having towered dead 200 yards behind the line, the Gun has no pleasure. On the contrary he believes he has missed it. I do not like seeing birds shot at out of range of the weapon in hand and although fluke kills of one pellet in the neck do occur, in respect of one's quarry it is not fair on the birds to be peppered at extreme ranges.

So we are back to choice and there are many excellent pheasant shoots where by skilful management the birds are presented in a sporting way. A pheasant by and large does not fly high. High birds are achieved by walking the pheasants up hill and the Guns down. On flat ground the use of strategically placed game crops, wind and trees all contribute to success. The principle is the same: pheasants are drawn away from home and so when flushed will fly purposefully back to their roosting wood. The Guns are placed at the sporting optimum point in between.

The high pheasant shoots do cost more per bird but are actually cheaper per shot fired to achieve the bag. I feel shooting should be let by the shot, not the bag. You can buy dead pheasants from a game dealer for practically nothing but there's no fun or sport in that. The value is in the excitement of the shooting which is better represented by the number of cartridges used. The sporting quality of birds on any particular shoot will still be subjective. A Gun or party of Guns will only take shooting regularly where they really enjoy the sport provided. What is important on any shoot is to ensure that game management and shooting days are run to be sporting, safe and ethical in line with the code of conduct published by BASC, the Game and Wildlife Conservation Trust and the Countryside Alliance. If not, then pheasants, whether high or low, could become just an academic argument.

Boys will be Boys

We love seeing enthusiasm for the countryside and the sports we enjoy in youngsters, for it is only through them that these sports will continue in the future. I recently met two young lads who had the enthusiasm and sense of adventure that I remembered so well as a boy myself, free to explore the countryside around my home.

I had received a phone call from a friend who farms south of Cambridge where part of the land is well inside the city boundary between a council estate and the mainline railway to Liverpool Street, to say there were a lot of pigeons on a bean stubble, which was soon to be ploughed. 'Would I like to have a go at them?' No difficulty in giving him a spontaneous reply, 'Yes – I can't go tomorrow but will be there on Saturday.'

'Look out for the public footpath on the north side of the field', he said.

I arrived in good time on the Saturday and cut an elder bush from the derelict scrub behind the council allotments. I then dragged it behind the car to the position I felt was the optimum for the strong south-west wind and yet away from the footpath. The field was about 300 yards wide and I was therefore 200 yards from the path and 100 yards from the farm track on the opposite side.

The forecast was for heavy showers driven on the strong wind and so I made a substantial hide based on an angler's big green umbrella positioned behind me. My son Henry was possibly able to come later and so I used poles and nets to make a spacious hide. This was completed with the elder branches, so creating an enormous new bush in the open stubble.

Pigeons soon started to come and my shots disturbed others on fields downwind which came on a line up to me. This was going to work unless conditions changed. One can never take anything for granted with pigeons. However it was not the pigeon coming to the field that surprised me but the number of people not just on the footpath but also walking the farm tracks. By mid-morning I was in the middle of a continual circus of dog walkers, joggers, mountain bikers, horse riders and mothers pushing prams. Saturday, I soon realised was not the ideal day for me to shoot this field! However the pigeon kept coming. Amazingly very few people seemed either to notice the new bush in the landscape or hear the shots on the wind. I had to set the decoy pattern to create shooting down the length of the field so my shot did not land anywhere near the footpath but I also had to keep a sharp eye as to where people were.

About midday the pigeons suddenly started turning away and not coming in to the decoys. I puzzled for a while and then decided to perhaps alter the pattern. As I came out of the hide I saw three young teenagers standing only 20 yards behind, two wearing white T-shirts and the third bright orange! 'Hello boys, how can I help?' I said. 'Oh we've just come to watch', they replied. I explained with surprising calm and patience that while they stood there in bright clothes there would be nothing to watch. I suggested they withdraw and watch from the burnt-out car on the sugar beet pad at the end of the field. A few empty cartridges in their pockets and off they went, watched for a quarter of an hour, got bored and disappeared back in the direction of the council houses.

An hour later the pigeon again turned away. This time I stood up to look over the angler's brolly behind me and sure enough there were two more boys standing there. 'Please mister, we've just come to watch.' I again explained the problem to these two youngsters and that I was in a hide made of camouflaged netting and taking every precaution not to be seen in order to fool the wary woodpigeon. 'Ah yes', they said, and off they went with more empty cartridges provided they did not tell any other mates. It had been a meeting with the first boys which had encouraged the intrepid second party of lads.

Three-quarters of an hour later, excited voices behind me warned me to again look behind. There were the two youngsters now dressed head to toe in cammo gear. 'After what you said mister, we went home and changed, are we all right to watch now?' Well what could I say but respond to such initiative and enthusiasm and welcome them into the hide.

Mathew and Leroy aged eight and nine respectively were like two excited puppies. I had them stand behind me under the umbrella, peering out through the netting for the pigeon coming. I explained what I was doing and they soon had their sharp little eyes competing to tell me of incoming birds. I told them to put their fingers in their ears when I put the gun up to shoot to protect their hearing. They referred to my hide as a 'den' and soon entered into the spirit of excitement and sport. I explained how one could tell by the result of the shot whether the bird was hit head, tail, right in the pattern or just winged. They loved it with morbid delight. 'That's dead all over', was Mathew's cry when a pigeon had flown into the full choke pattern.

Conversation with these two was no problem and they were very at home in the suburban countryside. I was honoured to be invited to see a dead fox they visited every day in a roadside ditch. It had obviously been hit by a car. I declined as politely as I could such a prestigious invitation to the hallowed shrine of the month-old dead fox. My score by now, about 4 p.m., was 174 on the clicker round my neck. To keep them amused when not smothering Conon, my golden retriever with fuss, we played mental arithmetic games of how many I needed to shoot to get two hundred. Eight and nine-year-olds have lots of fingers and thumbs, but not enough to solve such a problem. However they soon had a countdown and at two hundred we celebrated by sharing my packet of crisps and two remaining sticks of Kit-Kat. All this and still shooting a few latecomers before picking up.

TIME FOR DOMESTIC BLISS?

'February', my dictionary informs me, is derived from 'februa', the Latin for 'purification feast'. For most shooting men it is the month to restore marital harmony. Shooting widows of the past months have seen little of their husbands during the day whilst having the kitchen draped with wet kit and dogs at night and only loud snoring from the armchair beside the fire for evening company. The home has been turned upside down to accommodate shooting guests, shoot lunches and dinners, all a great amount of work, and what is the result? The dear husband is invited out on more days to return with more wet and torn tweeds to clutter her kitchen. Never mind the need for a 'purification feast', it is a 'reconciliation feast' that is needed.

Many game shots fly off to the sunshine in February and it is a good time for keepers to take a holiday after the long months of intense work. However, for many involved across the spectrum of shooting, February is the month with the cream of all sport – the pigeon roost shoot. This is when a group of true shooting enthusiasts get out in the middle of winter to strategically cover the woods on a farm or estate. Often this is one of the perks for beaters and pickers-up who have loyally attended every shooting day of the past season. It is also an opportunity for the young to get a chance of some shooting and so help kindle an enthusiasm for the sport which will be a passion for life. (Oh dear, another generation of shooting widows!)

Perhaps there is little new to write about roost shooting but I never fail to get a buzz of adrenaline when waiting in a wood, late on a winter afternoon and I see pigeons approach. Is one coming over my window in the trees? Will it be in range? Will it see me and jink off on the wind? There is such a thrill of anticipation in those moments. A successful shot is immensely satisfying

I dismantled the 'den' and they started collecting the bag of pigeons together – a slow business with only one pigeon at a time in each hand held by the tail. Two boys counting pigeon into sacks does not work either with chatter, mucking about and forgetting the first number they thought of.

We loaded the car and with a last cuddle for Conon off they went home happily with every pocket bulging with empty cartridge cases. I cannot think what they told their mothers but I know there will be two boys who will not forget the day. In a few years time they may or may not pass GCSE maths but for sure their enthusiasm will ensure they are countryside supporters.

and each evening will produce different conditions of wind speed and direction which will affect the flight and sport.

When the dead birds are retrieved it is interesting to open their full crops, which often burst on impact with branches as they crash to the ground. Oilseed rape will be the staple winter diet but, in my part of the world and elsewhere, ivy berries are becoming more and more a favourite. It is fascinating to see the amazing positions that a pigeon will get into to reach these berries. I watched a group of three as they fed on the ivy berries growing on a roadside hedge. They could simulate treecreepers or woodpeckers as they held themselves on the vertical, or even the blue tit as they hung underneath an ivy clump. Is there more ivy now than ever before? Maybe we have not noticed the slow invasion of so many trees, hedges and buildings by this multi-fingered, green triffid. Or is it the woodpigeon itself which is spreading ivy as the seeds pass through the bird and land encased in nutrient at the bottom of the tree in which it roosts that night? So, more ivy producing even more berries for future generations of pigeon. Has the wily woodpigeon learned from the farmer on whose planted crops he thrives so that now they, in turn, sow and farm their own ivy seeds as food for the future pigeon progeny? It may not be intentional but it is certainly a good example of a symbiotic relationship which ensures the survival of both bird and plant.

Whoops – I have diverted from that first exciting moment of an approaching pigeon. However, one's mind has always something fascinating on which to dwell, stimulated by the sight, sound or smell of nature in the depths of that winter woodland, whilst awaiting the first birds of the evening flight.

Oh dear – for the pigeon shooter February seems to have done little for domestic reconciliation after all.

A Bargain Hunting We Will Go

I am always interested in TV programmes of early man and our evolution. The common theme which runs through each period of whatever 'eolithic', in whichever millennia, is that survival has been due to man's success as a hunter-gatherer. This is still true today: man is the opportunist gatherer both in town and country. We all keep our eyes open for whatever will serve our needs whether as food or for home and family. It may be windfall apples or windfall share allocations, blackberries in the hedgerow or free offers at the supermarket. Most people may not choose to catch or shoot their own fish or fowl, but many, if not all, are appropriately called 'bargain hunters'. Man survives and thrives on what he can find for low cost, whether in cash terms or for energy expended.

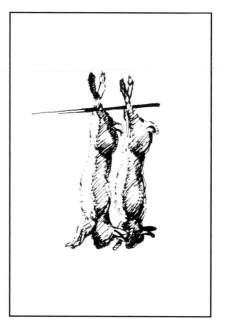

I remember so well when my son, Henry, was about 12 some years ago and we were on a father and son Scottish safari together. One day we sat on the south shore of Loch Ness eating our picnic whilst eyes scanned the loch for 'Nessie'. She did not appear but on the bank around us were both wild strawberries and wild raspberries. I don't remember what was in our sandwiches but we both recall the taste of those wild fruits enjoyed by man and boy hunter-gatherers.

The earliest cave paintings show so well the animals those primitive men hunted. They are depicted not as carcases in a butcher's shop, but with a mystical respect as quarry hunted not only for food but for the thrill of the chase itself.

In the case of shooting, we enjoy it for so much more than just the food it produces. If we ended a day's shooting when we had shot our brace we would often be home very early. So there is something else in us that values and is stimulated by the sport itself. The camaraderie of a group of 'hunters' is a big part of it, but not necessarily for the pigeon shooter, stalker or angler who enjoys the solitude of communing with nature, the fieldcraft of the sport and the challenge of their quarry. For all who shoot, the satisfaction of a successful shot is nothing if one does not greatly respect one's quarry. That respect in turn naturally creates a responsibility to ensure the quarry is retrieved and, if not dead, then speedily and humanely despatched. So hunter is also gatherer. The Gun has dogs and to back him up; a shoot has pickers-up. For them, the excitement of a shoot is the hunt with his or her dog to gather up the quarry. Therefore, the hunt and the gathering are inextricably linked. It is part of the teamwork, not only on a shoot, but across all the country sports.

When shooting, it is important to mark not only your own birds, particularly outlying or wounded ones, but also those of others. It is amazing how often a wounded bird will not be seen by anybody as it towers and falls dead 300 yards away. If others have seen it, then a cross reference of marks will make it easier to retrieve.

With experience one learns which birds are hit and pickable and which have only feather or skin shots. My personal rule is that I would never ask a picker-up to go for a bird I would not go to look for myself if time permitted. Respect from pickers-up is often hard earned. However, they soon learn who to listen to and who to ignore about a bird in the hedge half a mile away!

One day, shooting on the end of the line in a big wood, I had five birds to pick. A colourful, bearded country character was picking up behind me and appeared saying: 'I've got your four birds, Will.' I said I was sure there was a fifth; a hen about 100 yards behind by a particular tree. He doubted me but I insisted and we both walked back. After some distance he said: 'No, it's not here.' I urged him and his dogs on and sure enough, there at the base of the oak lay the hen. 'Will, you've got eyes like a shit-house rat', he said. I'm still working it out but maybe there is a compliment in there somewhere!

When pigeon shooting over a standing crop, I make a map of my location on a cartridge carton and mark each bird I shoot with an X. At the end of the day this helps considerably as I tiptoe about in standing corn or peas, only in the area I anticipate picking birds and so minimise damage.

Last January I was shooting in Suffolk standing on a field where onions had recently been harvested. I filled my pockets with those left on the surface, later to be ploughed in. Other Guns pulled my leg about my onion gleaning but I said pheasant and onion would go well in the pot together. I had enjoyed a good drive as both hunter and gatherer. Maybe I'm just primitive, but I'm proud to acknowledge my hunting gene.

Conservation with a Passion

As I sit in our cottage garden, looking out to sea over the North Norfolk Trust Reserve at Cley, an interesting question arises. Is it hypocritical to love birds but have a passion for shooting? I feel it is not but can certainly understand why it may appear so to those not involved in the sport. With the sights and sounds of birds on the marsh in front of me and those in the garden and woodland behind me, it is an appropriate moment to consider such fundamental philosophy and beliefs.

On the scrapes, avidly feeding in the shallows, were many waders. There were those who fed with long bills probing the mud such as redshank and greenshank, dunlin, whimbrel and godwit, whilst avocets gracefully swept their upturned bills from left to right below the water as they tiptoed along.

Both avocet and black-tailed godwit are great success stories for Cley. The extensive series of scrapes created on the marsh have produced optimum conditions of habitat as well as top ratings in the 'Egon Ronay' waders' good food guide. Avocets and black-headed gulls seem happy to nest at close quarters on the

Early Summer – The Lodge Lake at Hauxton (from a painting by W.G.)

islands where ringed plover and the odd turnstone share the margins with several species of duck and geese.

The whole place was alive and buzzing with activity, both on the marsh and in the air. A large number of sandmartins dived and dipped, definitely the spitfires of the bird world. Marsh harriers quartered the far reed bed whilst lapwings performed acrobatics in the air with happy, constant calling. Skylarks were incessant above with a multitude of micro-musical notes as reed and sedge warblers rattled and twittered in the vast reed-beds surrounding the scrapes. Bearded tits we did see, but the new arrival, the bittern, we sadly did not.

Bernard Bishop is an old friend and the fourth generation of Bishops as wardens of the marsh. Bill and I went with him for an hour or two to view the scrapes from their hides. Bernard's considerable knowledge and experience, compounded from great grandfather to grandfather and father, makes him unique. He and his father planned and made the scrapes, and the careful management of the water levels of the whole area is an art in itself. Bernard's eye soon pointed out that amongst forty or fifty dunlin, 100 yards away, there were two curlew sandpipers. Later he pointed out that one of the black-tailed godwits was actually a bar-tailed.

There are two sorts of bird sanctuary wardens these days: the 'Bernard' and the 'boffin'. Bernard is of the old school of keeper wardens. If there is a rogue rat, stoat or fox, he will deal with it, usually before damage is done. The 'boffin' warden will do little but write scientific, analytical reports after a problem to explain why nesting terns, avocets or whatever had been unsuccessful due to predation that summer. Surprise, surprise, in two years there is no colony of terns or avocets, just a lot of worthless words. Personally, I believe a reserve needs both a keeper warden permanently on site and a 'boffin' to record, but the reserve cannot thrive without the former.

Bernard and his father were both wardens and also part-time keepers of the estate surrounding the village where a successful, mainly wild game, shoot exists. Bernard is a man whose life is managing a national treasure, a reserve of international importance, with a love and great knowledge of those birds, common or rare, that it supports. Yet his passion is for shooting and he loads, picks up or shoots throughout the season. Nobody has a clearer, more balanced view of objectives. Think also of Sir Peter Scott – few men shot more wildfowl and yet he created better managed reserves for their future.

So often, it is the passion of the hunter that, through respect for his quarry and the habitat in which it is found, has actually contributed so much to the world of conservation. Is it the antis who plant trees, coppice woodland, and create ponds and wetlands? No, that is the work taken on with the enthusiasm and vision of shooting men. Appropriately, their organisation is named the British Association for Shooting and Conservation. Is there a BAAC – British Anti Association for Conservation? No.

Memories are Made of This

As I feed my pheasant poults in the release pens through the late summer, pampered on high-protein pellets and protected from predation by high wire fences, I look at these semi-tame birds and ask myself why I still find the pheasant such a special, sporting quarry. In the old days when hatched under broody hens or bantams, the young pheasants, as chicks or poults, looked sharp and perky, responsive to every cluck of their mothers – that way of rearing was a comparatively short step from the wild. The same young pheasants from incubators, brooder houses and intensive rearing facilities need all the management and care of any poultry but arrive from the game farm not only domesticated but with a death wish. They will try to drown themselves in drinkers, hang themselves on V-shaped twigs on bushes, or even poke their heads through the wire fence to allow a fox on the outside to bite it off. All such stupidities have happened over the years to my few reared poults. Any keeper will have a host of stories of equally incredulous ways in which their cherished young birds have committed suicide.

Yet for me, there is another side of the bird which commands my excitement and respect. It goes back to the fact that, as a boy in our small Cambridgeshire village, there was no keepered shoot. In fact, the only shooting was a once a year autumnal farmers' shoot which was based more on the conviviality of a day out together and a chance to chat about farming than any Edwardian battue. If, from the hollow of the spare wheel on the Land Rover bonnet, there was enough for a

brace of birds, a hare, duck or rabbit for each Gun, then that was a bonus at the end of the day.

So my Christmas holidays were spent chasing the one cock pheasant round the parish boundaries with Pincher, our Jack Russell terrier, and a borrowed single-barrelled .410. That lone wild cock pheasant kept me amused most of the winter and whether Pincher eventually caught him down a rabbit hole, or I shot him flying out of a clump of ivy, our bagging of such a trophy by dog and boy carried us through to the following winter.

Such memories are now a privilege from the days before I knew that the same bird was reared elsewhere in hundreds, or even thousands. Those early experiences not only taught me fieldcraft and honed the heart of the hunter but also taught me great respect for the pheasant. How could such a large, handsome bird, with highly coloured plumage, hide, avoid and outrun my terrier or outfly my gun? However, we did both learn to work as a team. Pincher would run on and work the pheasant back to me and I quickly learned to focus on my one chance of a shot, should there be one. It was a great way to learn to shoot straight as it was too much to consider missing after all the effort expended in achieving the opportunity of a shot. Now though, I am lucky to enjoy quite a number of days shooting and still each pheasant that flies towards me gives me a big thrill based on those boyhood memories.

So much of our sporting enjoyment is in the mind and in our anticipation. There are days when birds fly well with a good wind, or others when it is still and humid and they are moderate. There are drives where a single bird creates a great memory, whether shot or missed. However, all days are good days when out with a gun and friends. Ironically, a downside of good shoot management of mainly reared birds is that we arrive with a premeditated idea of the bag. Some people may be disappointed if it is less, and overjoyed if the bag is more than anticipated. To me this is a pity as it would be much more rewarding if we had no preconceived idea. All the more so, as a bag of half the expected number of birds in difficult conditions is so much more memorable than an excess bag when the weather is not conducive to flying.

I enjoy every season with the exhilaration of each pheasant as if it were that special boyhood lone pheasant. I hope my summer poults, now mature, will rise and fly high over a gap in the willows to give friends the same challenge of a single shot that carries on the wind and lingers in the mind.

Has Guns, Will Travels

Our sporting motto is 'have guns, will travel', and for a week, as August gives way to September, Barry and I go north to the Highlands of Scotland. For me it is easy. For my friend Barry, an Anglo-American globetrotter, it is just another transatlantic flight. He touches down at Heathrow, spends a day cracking whips and spouting wild creative ideas to those who run the UK end of his engineering business. While he is away the company grows from strength to strength and so they positively encourage me to take him for a week's shooting and leave them to get on successfully. I have to acknowledge this as the essence of good delegation.

So by Sunday evening we both meet in the bar of the Muckrach Lodge Hotel in Morayshire – a convenient central location for our two-man disturbance of the peace on estates that have keepers who can put up with us and game that can't.

As I write now I know that Barry is on the other side of the Atlantic, so I feel free to paint a sketch of his character. Our friendship is not an old one, and may not be a long one but now it is a real one. In many ways we complement each other as in the case of comedy duos – I'm tall and thin, he's short and.... I feed him the straight lines, he trips as he offers the punchline. Like schoolboys, we are rude to each other in jest. However, we share much of the same humour and most of the same faults, and actually such banter can only thrive in a friendship of mutual respect. In wine terms I would see him as 'new world', effervescent and precocious. Unlike the port he loves he is not a crusty vintage – though decanted into this world in 1947.

An unlikely friendship one might think but we bring out the best as well as the worst in each other. What we certainly share is a common passion for shooting and enthusiasm for all and everyone that makes it happen.

The exciting thing is that all sport at this time in the Highlands involves wild game. However, one of the many difficulties in organising a week of shooting is that wild game is seasonal in its success. That year we were to have started with two days of driven grouse but due to poor spring weather this was not a good season and so only one driven day was to take place. Our contact, Hugh, is a retired estate factor who has helped greatly in organising our grouse shooting and had kindly invited us to join his party of chums on the driven grouse day. The moor we shot was just as one dreams: a great plateau of heather in bloom broken by steep gullies with burns of sparkling water, tinged gold with peat, racing over boulders and stones as if late for an appointment with the sea. All this is surrounded by hills and with views of the Cairngorm mountains away to the east.

A flick of the skilled flanker's flag and a covey was turned towards the butts followed by a rattle of shots. A single old bird came like a bullet on the wind, a tilt of the wing and it jinked around a peat hag and through the butts unscathed. What was interesting was that there were either single old birds or good coveys of tens and twelves indicating that those that had hatched early had lost their broods but later hatches had got away well. A day of sixty brace left us exhilarated and the adrenal glands exhausted. We were late off the hill but the evening sun cast a wonderful glow on the glen below and our only regret of the day was not to stop and enjoy a dram as we imbibed that view.

Back at the Muckrach we were soon at the bar and ready for dinner. It is a hotel ideal for a sporting trip: comfortable but not chintzy; hospitable without pretence and with well-cooked good food, served with friendly humour. At the end of the day there is a comfortable bed that one can roll into having tripped over one's gun case – which once again is a reminder of the wonderful day.

Tuesday was again fine and we met Alan, the keeper, soon after 9 a.m. to walk grouse on the same estate. We drove miles up into the hills and the plan was to walk an area of the moor where, on an earlier driving day, disappointingly few grouse had been seen. Alan and his young, fit underkeeper went between us with their dogs and game bags. Conon, my golden retriever, and I took the left flank and Barry the right. Optimistically, it was arranged as a twenty brace day but that would normally have been for four or five walking guns. However, we soon started seeing grouse and in the thick heather they sat well enough for us to get within shot of rising birds. We soon had a few in the bag and, in fact, came across more good coveys than when the ground was driven earlier. By lunch time we had twelve brace laid out on the track as our game bags were emptied. A dram of McCallans all round and stories and banter flourished as we each ate our piece. Conon lay contentedly in the sun with his tail wagging – with Barry it was his tongue.

The sun was a joy, the breeze was stimulating and the air exhilarating. Barry was in very accurate form. He's not the fastest gun in the West but his over-under is heavily choked and he kills birds at great ranges. My style is more spontaneous as I am better at reaction shots than premeditated ones. It was a perfect day and our respective techniques again filled our bags in the afternoon. By 3 p.m. we ended back on the track and counted twenty-four-and-a-half brace of grouse and a snipe. A truly wonderful day for two musketeers. We thanked Alan and his mate and bumped our way down the track from the moor. On the crest of the hill, before we dropped down into the glen below, we stopped and put right our failure of the previous day. The late afternoon sun and view across the Spey valley to the mountains in the east was even more special than before. Barry had a bottle of port. The view just got better and better!

Wednesday could have been a problem as it was the day our second driven grouse party was cancelled. However, Hugh had phoned a few of his factor friends and found another walking day was possible, provided we were happy for a Canadian doctor to join us. Indeed we were and found that Alec was staying at our hotel so we had made friends before the day dawned.

Barry and I had been to this moor before and had had a great day out with Ron the underkeeper. Ron had the long shaggy tweeds of any traditional Highland keeper but the earring and hairstyle more commonly associated with New Age fans at the Glastonbury Festival. This year he had obviously come into contact with an Aussie contract sheep shearer, his long locks were away with the summer fleeces. He was still the warm character we remembered. Luckily Brian, his headkeeper, was with us so Ron's sense of humour that had walked us straight up a sheer mountain face last year was tempered and we set out across the flats.

Alec had not shot a grouse before and as his first bird was retrieved his camera was ready to record the moment. 'Click' went his camera and up from around his feet rose a large covey which disappeared over the skyline unchallenged. He shot well but the surprise element of walked-up grouse saved the stock being threatened. Twenty-two brace was our bag after another happy day. We had had a great variety of shots and felt we had earned each bird we had taken.

We left the Muckrach early on Thursday morning to travel two hours down the Spey valley before going into the hills to the south where we had arranged to meet Steve 'The Rabbit'. He had organised days of sport for us, in previous years, that Barry and I just love. We set off with our favourite keeper, 'one tooth' Garry, and his spaniel. He has a nose for the rushy meadows or 'parks' as they are known, where rabbits will lie out. His spaniel is brilliant, in fact almost too good and for the first hour he caught more than he flushed for us to shoot. However, with Guns versus spaniel at nineteen all we left the thickest rushes and the rabbits flushed earlier, giving us more shots. The fun of snap shooting rabbits is the excitement, as their agility allows them to twist and turn between clumps as they run for the safety of the stone dykes around the fields. In the afternoon Garry produced ferrets of all shapes and sizes and we went to open grass parks with isolated burrows or warrens every 50 or 100 yards. The rabbits bolted left or right for the next sanctuary and made interesting shooting as they ran over open ground. Each burrow may have had anything up to ten or fifteen rabbits living there but often it will take a team of ferrets to bolt them. Then, when the cupboard is bare, out come the ferrets into the daylight. Garry talked, whispered and whistled as he gathered them up. We ended the day with 120 rabbits in the back of the Land Rover – what sport at the modest cost of the equivalent of one brace of driven grouse. Actually over the years we have built a shooting fund from grouse day refunds when the anticipated bag was not reached. We count our wealth in rabbit days!

Then on over the hills to Aberdeenshire with my great pigeon friend Andy Hill and his cordon bleu lady, Kitty. We were thoroughly spoilt by their hospitality and sumptuous food. We are serious about pigeons but joke about everything else in life. Late summer pigeon shooting can be very special on stubbles and Andy has the shooting over a considerable number of small fields laid out like a patchwork quilt across the landscape. However, Friday saw us on an enormous field, recently harvested and with large round bales spotted all over it. He had seen a good

number of birds feeding there the day before but that day it was a bad forecast and although promising, success was not a certainty – it never is with woodpigeons. However, two main lines developed and we soon had Barry banging away whilst I was to be in a hide at the far end of the field. A good shoot developed there too, and later Andy also set up in a tree belt making a triangle of our three positions. In spite of steady rain it worked extremely well and we gathered nearly three hundred at the end of the day. Kitty was understandably unhappy as we were late for supper but what she called 'overcooked' seemed simply delicious to us.

Saturday was our last day and we travelled miles without finding a shootable situation until after 1 p.m. There was one good spot for Barry on the topside of the field and Andy soon had one of his special hides built against the fence. This worked well all afternoon. I went to a wood further up the hill behind where pigeon passed a gap in the trees. Not a busy flight and a few decoyed onto the grass field – but very sporting nevertheless.

We all went out to dinner at a local restaurant to celebrate a very special six days shooting of all wild species of quarry – what a thrill and what great memories. Is it because of or in spite of each other that Barry and I enjoy sharing such sport together as friends? Look out bunnies – we'll be back next year; we've still got several rabbit days in the bank.

SHOOTING SEATS

Other sporting writers have made rude comments about the various seats I have used for pigeon shooting. However as I shoot mostly from a sitting position I have experimented with all types. For most of his life Archie Coats was a 5-gallon oil drum man. This seat is fine but uncomfortable for long periods as it has no back. I then used an old wooden chair which John Humphreys referred to as the 'Chippendale'. This was comfortable but needed movement and I kept wearing out the seat of my trousers sliding to and fro and from side to side. Mark I, a secretary's chair, was a £5 scrap model which worked well but was too heavy to carry across fields.

Now Mark II is a very light plastic and alloy design from a commercial office supply shop. I stripped it down to its bare essentials by removing wheels and chrome decoration. It may only last two or three years but it is ideal and light enough to carry upturned, resting on my hip and held by only one hand. Alternatively a thin rope can be used to hang it over one's shoulder. So I now have the perfect seat which is comfortable, gives me a full arc of fire and is light to carry.

The French Revolution

In recent years each season produces some exceptional days' sport as French partridges use the wind to perform at their best. Certain drives give shooting as exciting as is possible of any driven game bird. As I have put my gun in its slip at the end of these drives I have been both exhilarated by adrenaline and yet exhausted by the focus and concentration these challenging birds demanded. It is time to reflect and acknowledge how in recent years the reared red-leg has become such an important part of today's driven shooting scene.

Nobody would dispute the sporting superiority of the wild grey partridge. The purist would say that neither the French partridge nor the French letter give the sensation of the real thing. However in today's world the latter produces safe sex and the former much good shooting. The catastrophic decline of the grey partridge over the past forty years has left a vacuum which has been filled by the reared red-leg. There are still some estates and farms where skilful keeping and sensitive farming have maintained a good stock of English against the odds of the national decline. However, recent years of cold wet weather in late June and early July have pushed the stock, even on well managed land, to the edge and in some cases to the point of collapse. Nevertheless, two or three kind summers could see the population recover, as was the case in 1975 and 1976.

The first major rearing of French partridges I heard of was at Sutton Scotney in Hampshire during the 1960s where Lord Rank supplemented the declining wild partridge stock with its reared brethren. I shot pigeons there with Archie Coats many times in the 1960s and 70s and can imagine just what a fine manor it used to be when birds were driven over tall belts of trees surrounding every field in rolling country.

It was about this time that, as the wild partridge declined, the price of partridges sold to the game-dealer increased significantly to the point at which an enterprising chap in the South decided to rear them commercially for the table.

Nobody then would have foreseen today's collapse of that price. He crossed them with the larger 'chukar' partridge from India and Pakistan. This cross produced a table-sized French partridge a few weeks earlier than the true French and so was even more viable and profitable. As these chukars were easily reared they were then introduced to shoots. However, they proved disappointing as they would run forever, rather than fly, and then tuck in to the hedge in front of the Guns. Those that did fly were usually moderate performers and people became disillusioned about rearing partridges at all. Then what turned out to be the best boost was that, as an introduced species, chukars were banned and all reared French partridges had to be true red-legs. For a season or two the tell-tale double black bar of the upper breast feathers betrayed chukar descendants but soon the breed became true red-leg again. The birds flew better and, given a breath of wind, could give excellent shooting.

Time has gone on and many moderate lowland flat pheasant shoots have now become extremely successful reared partridge shoots where sport is of a much higher quality than was ever the case with the pheasant. Ironically the secret is to drive them like pheasants from maize game crops rather than the traditional big, open field drives over a hedge. That still works if there is a cover or root crop, or even stubble from which to drive, but standing a crescent of Guns 80 to 100 yards back from a block of maize is surprisingly successful.

All depends on the wind. On still, bright days when the barometric pressure is high they will not fly well. A windy day with low pressure, even if wet, is a different story and many keepers and shoot organisers are now brilliant at using the conditions to make the best of the birds. Usually the answer is not to peg the drives but to stand guns according to conditions on the day. Then, if things go right, the Guns can be given the most exciting and testing shooting.

The reared French partridge has also extended the season and so contributed to the commercial viability of running a shoot. From mid-September until well into December, or even the end of January, partridges can be a very sporting quarry. So many pheasant drives are greatly enhanced by partridges that come early and give a sporadic rattle of shots before any pheasant is inspired with a sense of urgency to launch itself. Another point of credit in favour of partridges, whether wild or reared, is that they tend to spread giving most, if not all, of the Guns in the line a share of the shooting. Pheasants, on the other hand, often come on a very narrow line over just a few pegs.

How many partridges should one release? It seems to me that if you put down too few you only get half the days you want and if you rear enough then you get double the days you hoped for. As to what number is enough, this can only be a personal ethical or management decision. Whether few or many, it matters not – if the conditions are right the red-legged partridge will give quality shooting and memorable shots to savour.

A Bit of All Sports in the Hebrides

The police were called as soon as I arrived at the check-in desk at Stansted Airport. Was I a terrorist? No, just a law abiding owner of a shotgun which I was taking to the Outer Hebrides. The gun was checked against the numbers on my shotgun certificate and the atmosphere calmed. The officer carried off my gun to see it onto the plane. I was left hoping that they are as vigilant checking the bad guys. I was still a bit twitchy as I passed through the X-ray screen when the girl beyond gave me a steely gaze as if I were a criminal. Just that look made me feel guilty and I sharply put my arms in the air. 'It's all right, sir, there's no problem.' Behind the severe exterior she was rather pretty and I decided I might enjoy being frisked by her after all. It was then that a big security officer appeared from behind a screen and I changed my mind before any, new found frisking fetish got out of hand.

To cut a long journey short I was soon at Stornoway, greeted by Christoph Buxton and his keeper, Malcolm McPhail. The others in the party were mostly East Anglian mates and two of Christoph's sons, Ed and Richard.

Garynahine is an estate on the west coast of Lewis at the head of a sea loch into which a small salmon river flows from various burns and lochs higher on the moor. With salmon and trout fishing, grouse shooting over pointers, driven woodcock, wildfowling and fish from the sea, a season there is one of the closest spots to heaven while still on earth. All around the area is evidence that man thrived there 5000 years ago – they knew a good place when they found one; as did Christoph and his wife, Cilla, a few years ago when Garynahine came on the market. The lodge is ideal, being very comfortable without formality or pretence. Paul was the brilliant cook in residence but we had a rota for cooking breakfast and washing up. Teamwork was the key to successful indoor management and outdoor sport.

Saturday morning saw us as nine Guns split into three teams with Christoph as leader and floating Gun. We were to do the north wood beat which is a horseshoe of 300 acres of pines around a long loch. This wood is a strip fringing three sides of the loch, about 200 to 300 yards wide and nearly 3 miles long. It is divided into fourteen drives by rides or firebreaks where the forward three Guns stand. The standers then become three flank walking Guns on the top side next drive. They then walk down past the beaters to be walking Guns on the bottom next to the loch for every third drive. So the three teams rotate whilst the drives progress from one end of the wood to the other during a long day. Lunch arrives by rowing boat to a pretty spot where the burn runs into the loch.

It was a day of so many extremes: such beautiful views across the loch to the hills of North Harris, yet nightmare woodland for beaters. The pines grew originally to about 15 feet before devastation was caused by the pine beauty moth which killed

80 per cent of the trees. Now this dead, unbrashed area of uneven forestry with its solid web of criss-crossed branches and ploughed ground is not for the faint-hearted spaniel, let alone beater.

Malcolm's team must still carry the genes of those rugged Stone Age pioneers. Fuelled outwardly by cheerful spirit and internally by that of a more liquid form, they were amazingly effective and constantly jolly. The whole line kept up a constant prolonged call of 'Aay-up, aay-up', a sound that appeared to do more for the morale of the beaters than mean anything to globe-trotting woodcock. Nevertheless, they and their dogs performed impressively, considering the twelve-man beaters' line had to cover the 200 to 300 yard width of wood, as spasmodic woodcock were flushed and called 'forward', 'left', 'right' or 'back'. A communication system of whistles and three radios which were alive all day with the best one line humour and crack you'll ever hear – sadly most was not appropriate for publication.

'Guinness', shouted Russell from one flank, 'Razzle' or 'Shadow' came from Jim on the other. Malcolm was in the middle with Hemp, a spaniel reputed to be the sire of most others, pedigree or mongrel, on the island. Then out of somewhere appeared a colourful character, Phil, with his young lab, Digby. A keen environmentalist, it is said that he recycles the sweat wrung from his shirt as the alcoholic content is 100 per cent proof.

From the Gun's point of view, woodcock shooting is a most exciting day as one never knows if or when there will be the chance of a shot. When a bird does come sliding across the wood towards you, you have to make an instant decision: is there a safe shot or will it dive and fly past at head height along the ride or woodside, never presenting a shot at all. It is a sport of quick reactions: a possible shot one second is an impossible one the next. This is not the sport for the man who slumbers on his shooting stick awaiting a rise of reared pheasants. The chance of a shot is magic, a woodcock in the bag a triumph and for David his right and left a lifetime's dream come true. A nimble team of Guns accounted for forty-four on the first day and thirty-three from the south wood of over 200 acres on the second. This represents an exceptionally sporting way of skimming a light shootable surplus from the considerable number of migrating woodcock passing through the island at any one time. An extraordinary two days were enjoyed by all and we managed an average of ten to fifteen shots each per day to bag three to four birds. It is the sport of anticipation, every moment presenting the exciting possibility that a bird could appear. I was exhilarated after every drive, whether I had seen a bird for a shot or not. There was never a dull moment, always the sounds and sights of life and landscape tempered by the bright Hebridean weather we were lucky enough to experience.

On the following Tuesday morning we were back at Glasgow airport and the others in the party checked in for the London flight. With a certain amount of

embarrassment, I had to admit I was not going home but travelling on to Islay on the afternoon flight for yet more sport in the Western Isles. Yes, I did appreciate how lucky I was to have the opportunity of one venue, but to have another chance to compare sport on two islands was pushing Garfit luck to the happy extreme. Nick Fane, my host, met me on my arrival and had arranged to come up two days earlier than the rest of the party when he heard that I was already up north. So even more good luck as he had planned two bonus days: little did we realise just how special they were to be.

The house is a red sandstone Scottish baronial mansion complete with turrets and spires. It commands views over the sound of Islay to the paps of Jura. As there were just the two of us there on the first night we had an informal supper on our laps in front of a large open fire with enough logs to have employed a forester for a month. A glass or two of the Islay malt and plans were discussed for a day of roughshooting manoeuvres for a teal, snipe or woodcock on the morrow.

At 5 a.m. I awoke to the sound of a gale gnawing at the stonework serrulations of the tower in the top of which was my bedroom. By dawn the rain was lashing at the windows and the sea below the house was a cauldron of twisting and contorted currents topped by white, windswept spume. These were truly sporting conditions to stimulate adrenaline before the gun was even unlocked from the cabinet.

In full wet weather kit and buffeted by wind we met Donald James the headkeeper, known as DJ. In heavy estate tweeds he had little resemblance to other DJs but in common with Jimmy Saville, I found he had a magic way to 'fix it' – the sport on the estate anyway.

We went to hill lochans and bracken banks. I shot the odd driven mallard, teal and woodcock, walked-up snipe or rabbit. In the full force of the gale nothing made anything but a fiendishly difficult shot. We then did a manoeuvre on the reedy edge of a loch surrounded by trees where teal often rest by day: I waited behind a stone dyke having stalked into position. However, I spied the teal in a sheltered bay behind me, not in front, so I melted back behind a hillock out of sight. When Nick and Donald arrived surprised not to have flushed any duck I pointed out the teal beyond the ridge. Then some spooked and took off upwind but couldn't make it so climbed and curled high downwind over us. Nick and I both fired and one or two fell. The shots put up others and they took the same line. For ten minutes we had the most sensational teal shoot. Their speed, height and curl tested us severely but those shot travelled 60 or 80 yards dead in the air and then bounced on the waves as they hit the water. Nick is as good a shot as I know but we fired several shots into thin air. However, a successful shot was so exciting that we let out a yell of joyous exhilaration. We picked what we could of the teal, a mallard, a tufted duck and a pigeon but we had to wait until after our piece, eaten in the shelter of the boathouse, before retrieving the last three which by then had blown half a mile across the loch to the opposite shore.

Never have I enjoyed such a challenging sporting day. Of a total bag of twenty-six head there were twelve species and every shot of the day had a story worthy of an article in itself. DJ's black lab, Basher, had no bash left in him and Nick's wonderful pair of flatcoats, old girls at nine and thirteen, looked as dead as the leopard hearthrug on which they lay by the fire that night.

The following day was still wild but not as wet and I was offered a day stalking. The hind cull had gone well but a few more were yet to be taken off the hill and I had an exciting day with stalker Kevin Beard. I have stalked stags on a number of occasions but never hinds. I learnt a lot about the job with Kevin as we moved and spied, then crawled and slithered, trying to get in on the parties of beasts we found. Eventually success came: we were able to approach a group on high ground and the selected hind made a straightforward shot. Having said that, I am always relieved when the beast drops dead as I would hate to wound one. After gralloching it I took the liver, kidneys and tripe back down to the forestry below while the argo came up to collect the carcase. In the trees a plume of smoke indicated where a party of marines were holed up on a survival course. There was little wild food for them and they were really grateful for my contribution. The poor chaps looked drained and exhausted though they were at least dry under the polythene shelter they had erected with a fire inside. So they were comparatively warm and dry but famished.

That evening the rest of the party arrived, including Tal, Nick's wife, after a frustrating journey when the weather prevented her plane from flying the previous evening. Her mother, Piffa, is well known for her very amusing tales of a sporting lady. Tal has inherited not only her beauty but energy, enthusiasm, style and a genuine love of all the sport of the Highlands. Tal immediately took command as hostess making us all at home and so welcome. It was just wonderful to see the large house come alive with a party in the spirit and style in which it was built.

A happy band of pilgrims of diverse lives from the Navy, magazine publishing, haute cuisine London restaurants, city finance and landed gentry as well as yours truly, the itinerant artist. Such characters of the stage were complemented by wives and Nick's mother and aunt.

We set out for each of the three days shooting in full waterproofs and were treated to brilliant days of driven woodcock with bonus pheasant drives. The release of five hundred pure Michigan blue-backs on 18,000 acres is a management and keepering challenge. However, there were very attractive small pockets of warm conifers on rocky outcrops from which the birds flew exceptionally well. All drives, whether from conifer, hardwood or alder and birch cover, showed woodcock to test us all. Every bird had a sporting chance and each day produced mixed bags of thirty to forty head. Wet weather gear for the beaters seemed coincidentally to match the fluorescent orange of the council road men. There were many great characters but my favourite was old Walter, a retired headkeeper from the neighbouring estate with two good spaniels, a twinkle in his eye and many a story.

As walking Gun on one drive I met Margaret, the flank beater. It transpired she is Walter's granddaughter, and her boyfriend, Scott, is keeper on the estate next door. She too was covered from head to toe in unflattering waterproofs but with bright eyes and rosy cheeks. Surprising, therefore, to arrive at the check-in desk for British Airways next day on our departure to be greeted by her in a smart uniform. With a smile, she asked how I had enjoyed the shooting before dealing with my gun with efficiency and none of the previous suspicions. It is a pity that more airport staff don't enjoy beating and the countryside on Saturdays so shooting men can carry their guns as honest citizens, not suspected terrorists.

Time to be Noticed

The white pheasant is dead. For six shoots I had asked the Guns not to shoot it but on the seventh, our last driven day, I forgot. For Brian and me it had been our marker bird and throughout the season it was so interesting to see it in a game crop one day and at the other end of the shoot the following. It would return to feed and roost in one pen for a week and then be in the other pen for the next three nights. Sometimes neither Brian nor I would see it for days but then it appeared again like the prodigal son. That bird taught us a lot about the behaviour of those which we could not recognise individually. Now it lay with others, beside the long pond, shot on what had been the best drive of the day. There was a brief post mortem but no 'who dunnit' saga; Monsieur Poirot was not summoned. It was my fault for not giving clear instructions that day. The last driven day at Hauxton is with a few mates, all close friends who enjoy the surroundings and company and a shot or two at the cocks which have escaped the season. On this day we drive everything back to front and this surprises those clever birds who have previously lived off their wits and legs to avoid entering into the spirit of the sport for which they were intended.

Before end of season blues set in, it is a good moment to reflect. It is the time to acknowledge the immense amount of work put in by keepers on so many shoots all over the country: rearing, feeding and holding birds, and managing all that is involved in each day's shooting, all taking time, energy and expertise. Experiments with different pheasant breeds over the past few years have established which hold and perform best on each individual shoot for optimum quality. The wind has transformed many partridge days into exceptional shooting experiences. New friends have been made, old acquaintances rekindled. The shooting world is as full of characters as ever – most of whom are found in the beaters' wagon. If I have one regret it is that shooting days are giving the Guns fewer opportunities to meet the beaters and share the experiences of the day, let alone the opportunity for Guns to thank them at the end. At Hauxton I stage-manage this by laying out our modest bag so the Guns and my beater friends can meet and celebrate the sport we have all enjoyed. On many shoots this is difficult as Guns and beaters do not end up at the same location but even so, too many Guns fail to make the effort when the opportunity does arise to just say thanks. For Guns, the day may cost hundreds of pounds but to give thanks costs nothing. It is noticed and appreciated.

That point apart, it is becoming increasingly clear to me that we are now seeing driven game shooting at its zenith. Many people travel from all over the world to enjoy shooting in this country, testimony to the fact that Britain leads the way in shoot management. It is a big industry and foreign cash earner. There may have been periods of history, as in the Edwardian *Grande Battue* or 1980s corporate

slaughters, when quantity ruled. However, while there are some bad examples, as in any industry, the majority of estates and farms now manage a successful balance, producing enough birds shown at their best. That balance between quantity and quality is now at a peak.

The rearing of more birds is both ethically and politically unacceptable. There is scarcely the market for the amount of game produced now and any increase will lead to a further reduction of the market price and possibly create a collapse altogether. That scenario would immediately remove the argument that shooting produces a good food product at the end of the day. An 'anti' would argue that there is no correct scale of rearing an ethically acceptable bag – quality means nothing to him. We must be aware of the negative but more importantly acknowledge the positive. We not only produce the finest quality shooting, but in order to do this we create a landscape of beauty with habitat conducive to game and wildlife; and even urban antis would wish to preserve this, whether they choose to visit and enjoy it or not.

We countrymen and women are passionate about our sport. Whether a Gun, who is prepared to pay handsomely for the privilege, or a beater or picker-up, who works for no more than a token of cash, we are all here because we so greatly enjoy everything about the day: sport, countryside, wildlife, like-minded people all driven by a powerful belief that the countryside is important and its elements should be preserved. Pure water, fertile soil and clean air – without these there would be no life at all.

Maybe that white pheasant as a marker on my little shoot was symbolic in that it was noticeable. Each of us is like that white pheasant amongst the population: we may move about the world in mysterious ways in the eyes of politicians, but we should be noticed. It took a rally and two countryside marches to achieve it. Even though hunting was subsequently banned hunts survive with more participation than ever.

A Happy Tail

Conon in his prime

Some years ago I remember that with licky tongue and waggy tail, my golden retriever Conon welcomed me home with as much enthusiasm as a big, soft teddy bear. I had been away for twenty-four hours to hospital for an operation on my hand – no, not my trigger finger but the little digit of my left paw. I have had three ops on my right hand in the past for Dupuytrens Contracture, a condition which causes hard tissue to grow around the tendons of fingers and eventually leads to the curling up of those fingers affected. It seems to be really quite common and is thought to be partly genetic and partly physical. The genetic element is particularly common in Nordic races apparently. So maybe I have Viking ancestors, though I hope I am not feared as a wild-bearded, sword-swinging invader with evil intent on the local population as I move about the world to paint, fish or shoot. Maybe the Viking genes come out as I wait in a hide to attack pigeons or a butt to shoot grouse; perhaps it is then that ancient adrenaline flows again.

All dogs give their owners that wonderful welcome of unconditional love. There is no resentment or questions as to why you're late or where you've been; always totally forgiving and just an expression of pure joy at being together again. Hang on, I had better say no more or I may get co-opted as a counsellor for 'Relate'. Either that or sent by my dear, patient wife Gina for counselling myself!

Recently Gina showed me a passage in a book she was reading. The relevant section was referring to dogs mirroring the character of their owners. This being a somewhat deeper observation than the well-known adage 'like dog, like owner'. Labrador, golden retriever and springer spaniel were all included by the author in the group of dogs considered to be 'friendly and affectionate'. We all know that to be true of these, our most frequently seen shooting breeds, and I'm sure we are happy to think that they mirror those qualities in us. No wonder we all enjoy each other's company so much and develop such friendships on the shooting field.

I have had some good dogs, never more than one at a time as a car full of dogs and paintings do not mix. Painting rivers is a quiet, sedentary summer activity best suited to the temperament of labs and now my 'goldy'. I've never been brave enough to try a spaniel as they are so hyperactive that I fear more paint would end up on the dog than the canvas at the end of the day. So my painting assistants have always been the more placid breeds. Guinness, Belle, Dunton, Conon and now Scott all have just loved being out with me all day painting. Each one has learned to quietly sit or lie beside me for long hours whether in highland heather or lowland meadow. Just to be together is enough. However, they in turn all learned that the click-clack sound of my brushes being put down on the open lid of the paintbox means I am having a break or have finished for the day. At this point they'll suddenly sit up, tail wagging, as sharp as if I had fired a shot and there was a bird to mark. They know a break means a cuddle while I have a cup of coffee and maybe a walk along the river with a dummy thrown or hidden to retrieve, more love and fuss and then back to sleep while I work on for another hour or two. On warm days my friends Conon and Scott will quietly slide like otters from beside me into the shallows of a river or loch. There they will lie for ten minutes cooling off with water up to their shoulders. Then out they come and after shaking they settle back into position next to me.

My dogs have always been wonderful painting and pigeon dogs but impatient peg dogs. They'll be as steady as you like all day watching pigeons drop around them but the excitement of game and all the other shooting, dogs and action gets to them. However, as the book says, maybe they mirror my excitement out on a driven shooting day. The fact is they have all progressively developed better and better for painting and pigeon but become less well behaved on formal days. I think part of this is down to frustration as dead bodies lying on acres of bare soil or winter wheat can be seen for miles and present no challenge. So unless one is standing in cover or in a crop like sugar beet, there is little to interest an experienced dog. All my dogs have been full of energy, enthusiasm and drive which is good for long retrieves and picking a lot of pigeons from cover, but on a game day they would prefer to be away behind with the pickers-up with a chance to hunt for those wounded birds they have marked way back.

I admire those pickers-up, many of whom trial dogs and really have great control of them, even working a team. Nevertheless, my greatest respect still goes to the man who can handle a spaniel – hunting or picking-up they are a joy to watch.

However, I will settle for my mates Conon and Scott. We make a good team. I either sit them behind me in the pigeon hide or, if possible, 20 yards along the hedge under a bush to save their hearing. It is too late for old Conon who can no longer hear me tell him he's a lovely boy as he brings me another pigeon and I give him a pat. Wherever he sits, still though he be, his big, golden tail is wagging all day. That tail expresses his happiness and mirrors my own. I must read a bit more of that book.

Halcyon Days

Woodpigeon has just seen the decoys

Few things in life give as much pleasure as when a son enjoys his father's sport. It was therefore a wonderful day for me to sit in a hide watching my son Henry shooting pigeons on a field drilled with barley. Henry is of an age when one would have assumed that he had been shooting pigeons for ten years or more. Certainly I remember his first shots, taken with a .410, as clearly as I'm sure he does. However his young life of school, university and now working in London has not produced as many opportunities to go pigeon shooting as we would have liked. Nevertheless, he has developed into a competent shot at whatever quarry is on the menu.

The previous day we had visited the field in order to observe the flight lines and assess the best position for a hide. Reconnaissance is always important and in this case I wanted to check that the pigeons had not found another drilled field nearby. Some had, but the main activity was still on the original field and, provided the wind remained the same, one or two skimpy thorn bushes would provide the basis for a hide. It looked promising and we were quite excited as we returned home to prepare our kit and load up the car for the next day. However, I sometimes have to be careful that observation is not superseded by optimism; with pigeon sport is seldom certain.

The next day dawned and the omens were good, a rare dry day was forecast with a moderate north-west wind. Ideal conditions, but it was a cold wind and so we erected the old canvas horse blanket that I have used for years as a back wind shield. Then, while I set up other poles and nets, Henry cut some elder from the hedge at the end of the field. The buds had burst and this haze of young green leaves completed the extended bush producing a spacious hide for the two of us. The decoys were arranged as a casual feeding group to complete the scene and then I left Henry to carry on as I had to meet someone and would be away for an hour or so.

On my return I could view the situation from a rise on the track. Through binoculars I was encouraged to see many more pigeons out as decoys than we had started with. A pigeon swooped in from the left, there was a puff of feathers and it dropped dead. I heard the delayed noise of the shot as the sound reached me. I continued to watch as several more singles or small groups decoyed well and, nearly every time, one or sometimes two puffs of feathers heralded more dead birds to join the now impressive display of decoys.

I joined him in the hide and little encouragement was needed, his smile said it all. I had lent him my clicker and he had it hanging from a hide pole. He rose and shot another and clicked the twenty-eighth. I sat enjoying just watching, my arm still in a sling from my hand operation a fortnight earlier. It suddenly felt so much better that I slipped my bandaged hand into a free position and tried three shots myself. Not a tweak of pain and I happily realised I would be back in action earlier than I had anticipated.

It is interesting to watch others pigeon shooting from a hide. Most inexperienced shots tend to jump up too early. If anything Henry could help himself by rising to shoot a little earlier, as some pigeons came within range but drifted away without him being able to shoot. I talked a few of them in to give him the timing to create the optimum opportunity of a shot. 'One from the left approaching decoys, gently up now, steady, mount, shoot!' He soon learnt the benefit of slowly standing up, to not leave it too late and then jump up like a jack-in-the-box which alarms the pigeon and makes for a more difficult shot.

Henry explained that he had shot the birds on the left better than those on the right so I suggested that he adjust his seat and feet 45 degrees right of centre. This immediately helped and he was able to kill birds to his right more easily. His previously limited swing to the right was then opened up, creating a wider arc of fire. A good right and left at the next two birds proved the case and reminded me of a very spontaneous and amusing reply he gave when aged about four or five. I had asked if he knew the story of the two pigeons, to which he replied, 'Yes Daddy – BANG – BANG.' Now my story had been realised in his shooting.

As we ate our sandwiches Henry pointed to the clicker which at that stage read thirty-seven, equalling his previous best bag. The sandwiches went flying as another pigeon appeared from nowhere and obligingly hovered over the decoys while his gun came to hand. With a very focused shot it became a record statistic. Numbers aren't everything but Henry's total when we packed up was fifty-four. He had shot very well and no one can take away that fact. It was a perfect day shared together leaving memories that will live on – several stitches in the rich tapestry of life – and not a little pride as well as pleasure for old Dad.

A KEEPER'S NIGHTMARE

With the price of game so low one would have thought that the problem of poaching would be much reduced. However, a local farmer, having had odd pheasants shot from the roadside, tried a novel approach to solving the problem. At the farm entrance he put a notice: 'Please do not poach my pheasants – call at the house for a free one!'

I cannot prove it but felt that someone was filching one or two from time to time at night from the edge of my little shoot. One Sunday morning Brian, who helps with the keepering, and I set up a comprehensive spider's web of alarms on the vulnerable areas of the shoot.

That very evening at 10.30 p.m. a phone call came from the duty sergeant at the county police station. He informed me that one of his dog patrol officers had radioed in to say he had set off my alarms. The policeman concerned then phoned me to explain. A burglar had been reported in one of the houses which backs onto the shoot and as there had been a number of break-ins recently the matter was taken seriously – impressively so.

A helicopter with a heat-seeking camera and floodlights was in the area in minutes. My 70-acre shoot became the set for a Vietnam war film. It was flailed with the wind rush of the chopper blades, lit like a first division football stadium and scrutinised by the heat-seeking beam. Am I painting the picture of every keeper's nightmare scenario a few days before a shoot?

But more – the heat-seeking camera picked up a body hiding under a bush, so the dog handler was sent in to investigate. He followed foot tracks into the area, across the winter rape field at the end of the village, under our barbed wire entanglement in the bottom of the parish ditch and then into one of the neighbouring back gardens. However the helicopter pilot guided the intrepid officer and dog on in the direction of the body. It was then that he set off the first alarm gun. Shell-shocked, pale and shaking, the man and dog pressed on. However the pilot then radioed again to say that the alarm gun had made the heat focus of the beam run – it was no two-legged criminal but a muntjac deer!

Amusing though the incident was, I was impressed that the police are taking crime seriously and grateful to the officer for kindly reporting that he had set off the alarm. If our poacher was as stirred and shaken as the policeman, it will be an effective deterrent. However I do not expect a phone call afterwards to apologise!

What of the disturbance to the pheasants? Amazing to report, they tolerated the nocturnal theatricals and were all there next morning!

Tales from the Cabinet

Which is your favourite gun? This is a question I am asked from time to time. Like many who have a passion for shooting I have acquired a number of guns over the years and my answer to the question is, 'Whichever gun I feel like using on the day.' Hardly an instructive or authoritative reply but I love them all and enjoy each for its own beauty and character.

I am not a technical gun buff or an expert on their internal mechanics however, luckily, I know a man who is. Adrian Lemon who trades as Cambridge Gun Repairs was trained in the old school and was for many years the gunsmith with Gallyon & Sons in Cambridge. I do not own an arsenal of weapons or a collection of great value but the few I do possess are perhaps worthy of their brief story. My first shotgun after early teenage years with an air rifle was a single-barrelled .410. Not the prettiest gun in the world, well actually very ugly. An Italian under-lever opener, reminiscent of the cowboy rifle of the Wild West. However for me the countryside around home was not a canyon of whining ricochets as each cartridge was cherished and fired sparingly. Day after day of each school holiday there was an entry in an old school exercise book – 'Divinity' on the outside but with the destiny of game inside!

Most quarry was stalked and my respect for the wariness of wild creatures grew as my fieldcraft skills developed. So many firsts were with that little gun, including pheasant, grey partridge, hare, mallard, pigeon, crow, rook, stockdove (then legal), rat, squirrel and golden plover. No rabbits – sadly I grew up at the time of myxomatosis which totally devastated the population around here for many years.

My second gun, in my early twenties, was a splendid Charles Boswell double-barrelled boxlock 12 bore. Ernie Johnson, the great shooting coach at the Gallyon Cambridge shooting ground, saw the stock and action ready for rebarrelling in the workshop and kindly made a point of contacting me. It was £150 and has always been a favourite. I recall so many happy times with it – from my first day's pigeon shooting with Archie Coats in 1967, the odd opportunist shot when with the beaters on my patch at Hauxton, to shooting a full house of twenty-five pigeons with a box of cartridges one evening. It is unusually bored, true cylinder and full choke so is effective for quarry at any range.

In the late 1960s I was very lucky to see Spanish partridge shooting at its best on the planes of La Mancha and surrounding hills, as a courier, originally helping my friend Tom Gullick, who developed the legendary event it later became. I needed a pair of guns even if stood on the end of the line and so sold the few shares I owned and bought a pair of Lang & Hussey sidelocks for £1,500. Made in 1892 the actions were (and still are) in good order and they had just been rebarrelled. They are light and beautifully balanced and a joy to use. As they are now rather special I only use them for my few grouse and partridge double gun days. Aged 104 one of them achieved second top score in the first side-by-side championship in 1996.

I later bought a pair of Spanish workhorses. These were made by Pedro Arrizabalaga and were good, heavy, sound guns which I used for most pigeon and game shooting. They were a good buy for £1,600 in the late 70s though I spent another £200 on each being 'English finished' by Adrian who was still with Gallyon in those days.

A gun I own with more pride than any other (and yet it cannot be fired) is the Webley & Scott boxlock which Archie Coats bequeathed to me on his death in 1989. It is the gun with which he shot his long-standing record of 550 pigeons on January 10 1962. I occasionally used this gun when staying with him but in the end it was truly 'shot out' and therefore doctored so that no more shot could disturb its retirement. After so much use by its master all the chequering was worn away and the heel and toe of the stock were rounded like the stump of an old sailor's wooden leg. However, to me it remains a treasure and I am sure it tells legendary stories to the other guns in the dark of the steel cabinet like children telling ghost stories at night.

Two other loves are my grandfather's old hammer guns – both are Purdeys but they are not a pair. One was made for his twenty-first birthday in 1887 and he purchased the other later, although it was originally made in 1883 as one of a set of three. I had them reproofed and use the '83 one with its Whitworth steel barrels at least once a year for game shooting and occasionally pigeon shooting. Bored true cylinder in both barrels it throws the most even patterns and with 28 grams of No 7 shot it kills very cleanly. With this gun I became the first hammer gun European Champion in 2001. This was at the side-by-side European Championships and – to put the achievement into perspective – Richard Faulds won the main class with 92/100. In the hammer gun class there were only sixteen entries and my score was a modest 77/100.

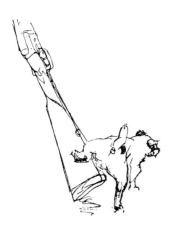

I later sold the pair of Arrizabalagas as I acquired a pair of 32" live pigeon guns made in 1907 by Frederick Beesley. They are splendid old boxlocks, heavy at 7 lb 13 oz but have become my favourites for all forms of shooting. (Their story is told on page 85 *Falling for a Beesley*)

All are side-by-sides and all give pleasure whether in action or just to hold and cherish. Often late in the evening I wander down to the studio and with gun in hand imagine a high pheasant flying along the ridge line as partridges skim across the purlin; knots in the pine door become coveys of grouse. A happy form of shooting as in the mind we never miss – dream on!

A Good Bag

What is the secret to the consistent success of shooting good bags of woodpigeons over decoys? It is a question frequently asked. Having recently realised, by counting back in my game diary over the last ten years, I find that I have averaged over a hundred pigeons a day. I therefore ask myself this same question to see if I can learn from the answers as I must be doing something right. One just does not get lucky that often. To share my thoughts may be of interest.

Firstly, the fact is that I do not always shoot a lot of pigeons and the average of a hundred birds a day is actually made up of days from only two pigeons, to my best day of 508. So I do get it wrong at times but in retrospect there is usually a good reason for this. Either the weather defeats me or something happens agriculturally that changes feeding patterns overnight. Some modest bags are on what I call 'duty shoots', protecting a crop at a vulnerable stage when there are not a great number of birds but the few that are feeding are being a real nuisance to the farmers. However, my experience enables me to read a situation reasonably accurately, to the point of estimating a potential bag within 10 or 20 per cent from my reconnaissance, whether it be twenty birds or two hundred.

I am fortunate to be in a good pigeon area. However, research has shown the density of woodpigeons to be high throughout the grain-growing areas of the British Isles. Yet in predominantly grass and stock country, as found in western Britain, the pigeon population is lower, or at best, patchy.

The big question therefore is, whatever the pigeon density, how do you get yourself in the optimum position for the best sport? I could say there is no easy answer but actually there is: you need to spend a lot of time on reconnaissance. I am fortunate to work for myself as an artist so I can detour on my daily journeys or make purposeful visits to different farms to keep watch on the current situation. Ideally I am one step ahead of the pigeons, watching the fields as the birds build up on them. If there are crops vulnerable to damage I then keep in touch with the farmer. Most of them are very co-operative as they know that when I shoot I will kill a fair few, and dead pigeons do not eat their crops. Bangers scare birds off but they either get brave and return, or eat other crops, so the problem is only postponed not cured.

Am I a pest controller or sportsman? Definitely the latter. It is the sport of shooting a wild bird that can produce every shot in the book which I find so exciting. However, the by-product of my sport is the important crop protection it achieves. It is the success of this that ensures my welcome on the farms where I enjoy my sport. So a constant link and symbiotic relationship exists between farmer and pigeon shooter for a win-win situation.

The key therefore is to get myself on the right field on the right day and in the right place on that field at the right time of day. Observation will give me all the answers. I do not need to see great flocks of pigeon but I do want to see a steady flow of traffic. Often pigeons will not need to be on a field for long to pick a crop full of food so there will be a constant coming and going over a number of hours of different birds, rather like people eating at a Little Chef. Sometimes there are a number of pros and cons for shooting a field from one of several positions. Usually I have a gut reaction early on in my decision-making and, more often than not, I am in the best place. If I make a hide and set up only to find that when I start shooting the flight line changes then I have no hesitation in spending time moving. I would rather be in the right place for two hours than the wrong one for four or five.

Do I have a routine which I stick to every time? Well yes, but routine should not be confused with recipe. The great challenge is that each situation is different and the fieldcraft must vary accordingly. Even during the course of a day, the conditions and corresponding response of the pigeon will usually vary, whether this is caused by wind, rain, sun or farming activities as a field is rolled, sprayed, harvested, etc. As in life nothing stands still and the world is constantly changing – so must the pigeon shooter. Another advantage of working for myself is that I can to some extent shoot a promising field on a day when the weather looks suitable. I always keep in my mind the outlook forecast for the week and particularly note the wind strength and direction.

So… I have arrived on what I have observed to be a shootable field, on the right day and an hour before I can expect the main activity. This may be at dawn, mid-morning or, in the hot weather of mid-summer, it could be late afternoon. I try to give myself the time to shoot for as long as the pigeon dictate. Often a shoot will be for five hours, sometimes for seven, eight or nine. Frequently people say they shot forty in a couple of hours. Well at twenty an hour it could have been a hundred day if they had been there longer. Often things start slowly and I question whether I've got it wrong. A steady shoot over a long period may not be a hot spot but the protracted sport gives you time to savour the moment and all the birds, plants and wildlife with which you share that special day.

On arrival the next stage is to set up decoys where pigeons expect to see them and a hide where they do not expect to see me. Whether in a hedge, on woodland edge or from bushes dragged out into the middle of the field, I like to get to where the pigeons want to feed. It all sounds so obvious but I often see people shooting from a tree or a hedge conveniently close to where they can park their vehicle, rather than slog out to the far end of the field where pigeons actually want to feed. At times it is hard work carrying kit a long way and hopefully carrying a sack full of birds back again at the end of the day. I do not travel light as I have spent too many hours in uncomfortable hides without a seat or taken half the day to shoot enough pigeons to make my decoy pattern convincing. I weighed myself once with gun, rucksack, decoys, cartridges, nets and all my kit and found that my eleven-

and-a-half stone was matched by the total load I carry out. Half a mile across a sticky ploughed field or along tramlines in standing corn on a hot summer's day and I question my strategy. When I carry it all back in two trips, with fifty or sixty birds in a sack each time, I may be exhausted but happily so.

Again I am frequently asked what is my kill per cartridge ratio? I can usually side-step that and say 'sufficiently effective'. Since a boy, with my first single-barrelled .410 and my lone sorties around the hedgerows of the local farm, I have always recorded the quarry accounted for and the number of shots taken. I still have a morbid statistical streak and know how many cartridges I take out and therefore how many I return home with. Thus each gamebook entry records the truth, good or less good. As this depends not only on my performance on the day, but the quality of the sport, it is the worst averages that actually indicate the best days' shooting. As I shoot I find that I am clicking, on the counter round my neck, about twenty pickable birds per box of cartridges fired. I would not expect to do that in a strong wind or on a high flight line shoot. Some might say I pick my shots and certainly I have developed an eye for the killable moment of truth. I rarely waste cartridges at birds out of range and that range for my side-by-side, choked quarter and three-quarters has a maximum of about 50 yards. I reckon to take on anything at any angle, speed or height that I see within that range.

There is no escaping the fact that to regularly shoot good bags of pigeon one has to shoot quite straight. Simple arithmetic will show how many opportunities one needs to shoot a hundred pigeons based on an individual's cartridge to kill average. A pigeon guide I knew once had a client who always complained that he was never given a chance of a hundred day. One time after he had fired nearly four hundred shots for fifty-something birds, he complained again about not having the hundred day opportunity. My friend told him in old-fashioned words of two syllables that as long as he had a hole in a certain part of his anatomy he would never shoot a hundred pigeons! The client is still awaiting his first hundred day but not with that guide.

Shooting pigeons is an acquired art and I have seen good game and clay shots defeated by this sporting bird. The fact is clays and driven game do not radically alter course in flight like woodpigeon do. Pigeon turn, jink, dive, flare and in a moment an easy shot can become an impossible one. Such is the sporting challenge of the bird and the reason why I love and respect it above all other quarry.

Have I said anything new? I doubt it. However there is something new to learn about the art of decoying pigeons on every shoot. I also know I have never had a day, irrespective of the bag, that I have not enjoyed immensely. It is sport that in Mr Kipling's words is 'exceedingly good' – even if you don't have one of his cakes in your lunch box.

Falling for a Beesley

After a day spent with a Beesley live pigeon gun and an expert woodpigeon shot I admit to coveting my neighbour's shotgun.

My passion for pigeon shooting does not diminish with age. In fact, on the contrary, I love the sport more than ever. However I do get a few twinges in my neck and shoulder which may simply be the maturing of middle-aged bones, cartilage and muscle. On the other hand I have recently been giving thought to the situation and believe my comparatively light side-by-sides may not absorb as much recoil as would a heavier gun. I do not really want to use an auto or over-under which would absorb much of the recoil but I have been playing about with the idea of using old live pigeon guns. These were made for competition shooting so popular in the mid-nineteenth and early twentieth centuries. The guns used were mainly side-by-sides weighing 7½ to 8 lbs usually with 30" or even 32" barrels. With guns of that weight recoil is negligible.

It was therefore of great interest when talking pigeon chat, as one does with fellow enthusiasts, to hear that Peter Schwerdt had not only one but two Beesley live pigeon guns. Now Peter is not known for doing things by halves. He is a somewhat larger than life character who takes himself very seriously one minute, only to play the buffoon the next. When pigeon shooting is the subject then he is in serious mode and he too had gone along the live pigeon gun route. He usually uses an over-under but he saw a Beesley for sale and liked it enough to buy. This was a 32", semi-pistol grip, boxlock with Greener type action locking bolt. Although a 12 bore it is a 10 bore action. It is number 1999 made in 1909 according to Fred Buller of Beesleys who kindly looked up the records. Though a boxlock it is not a grand gun but it is a beauty and well finished in every way – a great find.

Amazingly at about the same time Phil Beasley, himself a well-known pigeon guide and pioneer of the Pigeon Magnet, had also bought a Beesley live pigeon gun, needing no better reason than it being made by his namesake. So, when Phil Beasley and Peter Schwerdt got together to discuss their two guns they found that they were absolutely identical. More than that, they were actually consecutive numbers, Phil's being 1998. Both were made on the same bench by the same man and to all intents and purposes are a pair. Although originally sold for £40 in 1909 I suspect it cost Peter many times that to acquire Phil's gun and create the marriage. The coincidence is amazing enough but even more so when it would appear they were only the two live pigeon guns of that type and grade made by Beesley at that time.

So, after that happy tale, the next idea that emanated was for Peter and me to have a day pigeon shooting together, each using one of these splendid guns. The day dawned and I set off for Surrey, as Peter had found two adjacent fields of layed wheat which looked promising. However that had been a week prior to the day we met and the pigeon had moved on to rape stubbles on land over which he did not have access to shoot. So he suggested a brave thing, which was to go to a new farm on which he had just got permission to control pigeon. After half an hour of driving along the M25 and many tiny lanes we came to a pigeon shooter's dream farm – many small fields with big hedges, each with prominent 'sitty' trees and surrounded by acres of ideal pigeon habitat.

Several of these small fields at the far end of the farm were rape stubble and there were a number of pigeon already either on the ground or sitting in the trees. We watched for a while, having to do a rather hurried reconnaissance on new ground, which is never easy. Interestingly the main flight line was of pigeons coming downwind to the area. As pigeons will usually work their way upwind it was a case of having one gun on the downwind line and another on the upwind field which was two fields away. However, to start with and to enjoy the guns together we both began in the downwind field where I continued for the rest of the day. A spacious double hide was built in the shade of overhanging oaks.

So the moment came to handle one of the Beesleys. Both have been 'Teague' choked and the one I was to use was with half and three-quarters. The first observation was that in spite of the gun's weight being around 7 lbs 13 oz and the long 32" barrels, it handled beautifully with the balance and life of a much lighter top grade game gun. I raised it to my shoulder a time or two as a dry mounting exercise and the cast and stock length seemed perfect for me. I am not used to a semi-pistol grip but that combined with the long barrels and weight gave the sensation of a very pointable and controlled gun to swing.

The pigeon were slow coming and not convinced by our decoys. They were either passing by behind us or failing to negotiate a rather tight access to our field. It became obvious that we had to try a new strategy and quite rightly Peter suggested we double the distance of the decoys and magnet out from the hide. This proved to give the birds more confidence and we started to get some shooting. Peter uses Winchester Weston cartridges which are only for big boys with big guns as their heavy loads kill at great ranges but they would kill me and shake my normal gun to bits. I used my usual Gamebore Clear Pigeon cartridges. These were barely noticeable in the heavy Beesley.

Peter had acquired some new Realtree cammo gear at the Game Fair. I had to laugh but admit it was very effective. It is made from their hide-screen material which is very light scrim with brown leaf-like pieces of cammo which flutter in the breeze. This was made into a jacket and trousers, rather like camouflaged pyjamas. Robin Hood and his Merry Men would have loved them though, had Maid Marian worn the matching negligee, they would never have seen each other in the forest by day or night. The Realtree alternative to safe sex is no sex. Literally out of sight out of mind, as the saying goes.

Peter then left me and went to the upwind field where he had made a hide earlier. The sound of the Westons soon echoed downwind and he was clearly in action. The wind was strengthening at the time and made for exciting and testing shooting. The Beesley was a joy to use and I was quickly building confidence as wide or long birds collapsed dead. In fact I found the combination of weight and long barrels gave me a very controlled aim. I don't like using the word 'aim' for a shotgun but the effect was very positive. I was consistently killing birds up to 10 yards further out than I would usually take on. By the end of the day I decided I would happily swap it for any one of my guns, I had fallen in love with it. However, quite rightly Peter was not to be persuaded to part with either. If you get bored with them Peter, let me know!

Sport continued until about 6 p.m., never hectic but always with some interest and occasional bonus as inquisitive young crows came within shot of the Beesley but did not live to eat eggs next spring.

Malcolm, Peter's friend, who is the keeper at the first farm on which we were to have shot, kindly arrived to help pick up. I had seventy head and Peter had accounted for eighty. A combined bag of 150 on new ground without prior reconnaissance was a good day, especially as while my dog, Conon, hunted for the last bird or two along the hedge I came across the site of another hide very recently used. Peter also found the same in his field, so no wonder the birds were spooky and shy, having been shot there within the previous few days.

With the last of the kit loaded in the vehicles a storm brewed ominously. As we parted a rainbow lit the sky and a rumble of thunder replaced the banging and booming of the Beesleys echoing across the countryside.

Focus on Gold

Soon after he won the gold medal in Australia in 2000, I had the pleasure of meeting our British Olympic hero, Richard Faulds. Not only is he an exceptional shot but a great ambassador for the sport of shooting, both competition and game. A young man, quiet and modest whose responsible attitude to shooting and the politics that surround it is an example to shooters and non-shooters alike.

A year later it was therefore the making of a story for future grandchildren to find myself honoured to stand beside the great man at the award ceremony of the European Side-by-Side Championships, he having won the hammerless class and me the hammer gun class with grandfather's 1877 gun. The fact that he had a score of ninety-two against many competitors and I had seventy-seven against few, puts the event in perspective. For me a one-off life story, for Richard yet another championship title.

I spoke to Richard afterwards and conversation turned to pigeon shooting, as it does. I asked if he would be amused to come and have a day with me if I could find something of interest. For the Mr Cool, who contained nerves and emotions until the last pair of the Olympic shoot-off, to be so enthusiastic with open-eyed excitement at the prospect of a pigeon shooting trip, took me by surprise. Yes, he loved pigeon shooting and would be there.

It so happened that the following week a large rape field had been harvested and a flight line had developed between it and the cement works' quarry a mile to the east. This is an attraction for pigeons but as to why I am still unsure. It may be water but more likely calcium, as the pigeons can regularly be seen sitting on the chalk spoil heaps.

Along with the birds which respond to decoys on the surrounding cultivated ground an extra sporting element can be provided by a prevailing westerly. In these conditions pigeons make both upwind and downwind flight line shooting. That was Plan A. Plan B would be to shoot the large rape stubble itself which would produce a larger bag but in normal conditions not such interesting shooting – for the Olympic champion I wanted to offer something challenging.

The day dawned, a bright and breezy forecast but would the wind back towards the south? I drove round on a final reconnaissance early that morning. Even then the birds were moving and the wind was right.

After a quick coffee at home, off we went to the venue only a couple of miles away. Being in good time, we made a detour and stopped at the top of a hill. After a short walk Richard was amazed by the sight of the cement quarry ranging across 100 acres and more than 100 feet deep. Through binoculars we could see a few early birds sitting about and others coming and going. We then went to watch the flight line to the rape stubble. The good news was that there were quite a good number of pigeons moving but the bad news was that, as I feared, the wind was backing to the south. This in effect was then blowing across the flight line with the result that the pigeons were dispersed over a front of 400-500 yards. To set up and shoot this would not work as we would not cover enough of the fragmented pigeon traffic.

So Plan B came into play. This meant constructing a large double hide in what I had observed to be the key position in the middle of the 105-acre field. This was achieved with poles, nets and a background of elder branches cut and towed into place from the nearby woodland edge. I set up the decoys, in this case also using a pigeon magnet, to draw birds to the area and hopefully give them confidence to approach the new feature in the landscape, our hide.

I then left Richard to shoot while I watched from a distance to see how the pigeons reacted. If they headed for another rape stubble over the hill then Plan C was for me to go and shoot there to keep them off. In the event things went well and Richard was soon in action with his Beretta auto and Express Supreme 28 gm 7.5 shot cartridges. This small shot may win him championships but would it be too frail to kill woodpigeon I wondered? With his accuracy and the Beretta's full choke, the puff of feathers I saw drift away on the wind as another pigeon fell dead, sometimes 50 or 60 yards out from the hide, demonstrated that my fears were unfounded.

Having assessed that the situation was working well, the hide was in the right place and only a few birds were interested in the other field, I joined Richard. When sharing a hide, I like to actually build it as two hides so that there is a net between us and each has a clear and safe separate arc of fire. Safety is always paramount in such situations. I had set the hide cross-wind so the birds would mainly come into Richard as they approached upwind from his side. However the wind became stronger and pigeons came flaring on past us, not decoying but producing even more interesting and testing shots.

We soon settled to a rhythm as it became clear for whom the next shot was possible. He had pigeons passing wide out to his left and was killing some great challenging birds. From my angle on his right I could see over his shoulder as the shot went true from muzzle to target, up to 60 yards out. I had some fast downwind grouse shots as pigeons came round the shoulder of the hill and then saw the decoys. It was a joy sharing, our teamwork was working well and pigeons were dropping dead out of the sky at all angles.

Richard said he thought our shooting must look a pretty picture from the road. The quality of the shooting in the wind egged us on to take birds at all challenging angles, speeds and ranges. The three shot auto was at times used fully to account for one jinking downwind bird. Some birds came high, responded to the decoys but were spooky about our hide and turned away still high, to drop back on the wind. I assessed each but felt none were on for a shot. However Richard decided otherwise and took the last bird killing it cleanly half as far out again as I would have thought shootable.

I asked Richard what training, practice or mental preparation he needed to produce consistent top class competition performances. Game shots can miss a bird and just swear at the gun, cartridge, or dog and expect another chance in a minute. However for world-class clay shots, it is more like a test batsman at cricket – if you miss you may well be out.

Focus and concentration are areas in which Richard found great help from a

sports psychologist. The method suggested is of help to us all and yet fundamentally simple. Think, worry, dream of whatever between shots but have a physical moment, which for Richard is the click of the gun closing prior to his next shot, and from that moment focus on the target. This minimises wasting energy unconsciously when waiting between shots but tunes all senses to a peak for the short period it needs to climax. For game shots I suggest this could be the moment of pushing off the safety catch or the time you mentally say 'yes' to the bird being yours to shoot.

I gave his advice a lot of thought and used it successfully a month later in a foolish bet I had accepted after a few drams late at night. My Anglo-American shooting friend Barry loves a bet and has a mind for nocturnal mental arithmetic exercises – one of the reasons he is so successful in his international engineering company. His £100 bet was that he'd shoot more pigeons than me next day irrespective of bag based on his 1.7 for my one shot.

He is a good average 50 per cent man and it was not until next morning when

I awoke that the implication dawned. If he shot say 170 shots and picked eighty-five pigeon, I had to do better than eighty-five with my hundred shots. All morning he chuckled and jumped up and down with the joyful anticipation of taking £100 off old Will. We drew for hides from the two positions and the pressure was on but he did not know about Richard's advice and I applied the counselling.

Pigeons decoyed well and I was delighted to get the first ten with ten shots, twenty with twenty, thirty with thirty. This was too good but each bird that came died. Whether high crows or jinking second birds off right and left, none could escape the line of concentration or shot. I hoped Andy Hill, with whom we were shooting, would come to pack us up but no, 5 p.m. was the allocated time – forty, forty-seven, eight, nine, fifty straight on the dot of 5 p.m. Never before and, I suspect, never again will I do it but what a lesson in concentration.

Was it the thought of loosing £100 or Richard's advice? Whatever, it certainly worked on the right day. I lost three of the seven outlying birds that tottered back to the wood but picked forty-seven. Barry had got what he thought he needed, fifiteen birds picked from his thirty shots but with dismay reluctantly pulled five £20 notes from his back pocket. I cannot think of anything worthy enough on which to spend my prize, though a drink of thanks for Richard will be high on the list.

After the exciting day sharing a hide with Richard we did not have a cartridge kill percentage to write about but the 216 birds we picked were all from the greatest quality of sport. Maybe the moral of my story with Richard Faulds is that a young dog can teach an old dog new tricks.

Best Foot Forward

It was not until I took my father-in-law to the West London Shooting School and met Percy Stanbury, forty years ago, that I realised there was such a thing as shooting style. I was in my early twenties and had never been to a shooting school. I had learned to shoot with a .410 around the hedgerows on the farms near my home and to me, shooting with a shotgun was an extension of shooting with an airgun. I had taught myself to snap-shoot with my air rifle at static cans and then at them swinging as pendulums on a string hung from a tree. It was therefore a natural progression to shoot moving rats and squirrels with the air rifle, before being given the .410 shotgun.

Percy Stanbury however showed, by just demonstrating footwork and gun handling, that shooting was an art. Almost like a ballet dancer he moved with a rhythm and balance, man and gun were as one, at all times connected and related to the target. This was style and what a lesson it was.

I later realised there were other styles and as Percy Stanbury epitomised that of shooting with the weight on the front foot, Robert Churchill, of Holland and Holland, was the exponent of shooting on the back foot.

In the shooting field I now see many examples of each, as well as those in-between, who have their weight fairly evenly distributed. Clay pigeon shooters tend to shoot in this way. It is successful for them as they can set themselves up for a clay of known angle, speed and trajectory prior to calling for the bird. This of course is not as easy for the game shot who needs to keep his footwork and body moving in response to an ever-changing variety of shots on any drive. After all, this is the fun and excitement of game shooting. The front foot Stanbury style tends to best suit the tall slim chaps and the Churchill back-foot style favours shorter men of more chunky proportions. However, what each shooter of good style will display is nimble footwork to enable a unity of movement through their feet, hips, shoulders, head and gun relative to the quarry whether feather in the sky or fur on the ground.

I was impressed the other day on a partridge shoot when the elderly Gun on the next peg responded fast to birds and turned so well to take a second bird behind, having killed the first in front. He did so by moving his feet and body with agility that many younger men would have been proud of. Unfortunately as experienced shots get older some slow down and can become a concern to their neighbours.

Clay shooters are usually the safest shots in the shooting field, as safe gun handling is rightly part of this very strict discipline. I watched a well-known clay pigeon shooter prepare to shoot a bird which then went to his neighbour and so he politely did not fire a shot. In true clay shooter style he then broke his gun and in the open position rested the muzzle on the toe of his boot to await his turn for the next bird as if shooting in a competition. This would seem odd to game shots but was certainly very safe.

Youngsters or ladies taking up shooting are frequently seen holding their guns at arms' length when mounting them to the shoulder. The weight of doing so then leads them to lean back to compensate and makes for a poor gun mount and the gun is all over the sky on its way to find the bird. A disappointing miss is usually the result. Watching an experienced good shot, the gun is held up and close to the body to enable ease of safe footwork to turn left, right or behind with minimum effort.

Hands are important, and for balance and manoeuvrability side-by-side shots tend to shoot with a longer left arm than those using over-unders. A gun will handle best when the weight is evenly distributed between the hands. This will enable the gun to come up to the shoulders and be cleanly mounted, without any see-sawing caused by the left or right hand needing to work unevenly to lift the barrel or stock disproportionately.

We probably all think we shoot with better style than we actually do. Watch yourself in a mirror or on video; often a disappointing experience but one from which to learn. I will continue to watch and enjoy those who perform with effortless rhythm. Their footwork is always early in anticipation, their body and gun co-ordinating with the bird as the shot is fired and you know the bird will fold dead in the pattern of the shot.

Hopefully it is your style I'm watching with admiration.

Mad Dogs and Englishmen

An anglers' umbrella sir?', quizzically responded the British Airways man, having enquired about the long thin package I was checking in with my suitcase. 'To Brazil in the dry season – sir?', he continued with one eyebrow raised and an increasingly disrespectful emphasis on the 'sir'. I felt the beady eye of suspicion rising from the depths as a salmon responds to a fly. No it was not any form of weapon of evil intent. Yes I was an artist going to paint in Brazil where the brolly would, I hope, act as a sunshade. A moment of eased tension before he turned like the salmon and returned to his lie behind his desk downstream of the oncoming flow of passengers.

Cattle country – Brazil (from an oil painting by W.G.)

Twenty hours later I was bouncing along orange dust roads in a pick-up truck driven by James the farm manager with whom I was staying. During the journey he filled me in about the agriculture of the area. The company he works for owns ten farms in Brazil, predominantly cattle but in recent years sugar cane has become an important crop. Eventually we entered his farm with the righteously inspiring name of Cherubim and we were in cattle country.

The only thing slightly cherubic about James is his face, otherwise he is built more like the Nelore bulls he rears. They are the white cattle with humps on their shoulders seen in Indian films. However, unlike those in India which look emaciated, these are large with fine conformation, being selectively bred. This is big country, not ranched as open prairie but paddock-grazed on special coarse grasses introduced from Australia. Each field is up to 800 acres and each farm 20–30,000 acres. We went for a four-hour drive around the northern end of the farm, for me to soak up the atmosphere and get a feel for the character of this particular landscape. It was greener than I expected but this is because it was at the end of the wet season, after 50–60 inches of rain had fallen in three months. This was rolling country spotted with odd random trees giving the impression of a vast parkland landscape. When the area was cleared of scrub forest, the main specimen trees were left for shade – and for me, beauty.

Painting was a test as the daily temperature soared to 37°C in the shade. The sun rose at 7 a.m. and set at 6.30 p.m. It sizzled everything in its rays from the moment it first shone and lit the world. I was lent a battered pick-up which was my travelling friend each day. The umbrella pole was stuck in a hole in the spare wheel rim on the ground as a base, as there was no way the point could penetrate the concrete-like ground. My fear of rattlesnakes, scorpions, malarial mosquitoes or unknown plagues of pestilence were fortunately unfounded and all things beastly were away on a sabbatical. Just a pair of vultures circulating above on thermals made me wonder if they knew something of my future that I did not.

The sun bore down relentlessly but in the shade I kept to a disciplined plan for each day to work from 7 a.m. until midday, then a break, swim, lunch, siesta and then work from 3 p.m. until 6.30 p.m. With a plentiful supply of water bottles in a cool box I avoided dehydration and maintained concentration.

How have I written so much without a mention of a dove, duck or pigeon? Well, I was of course watching out of the corner of my eye at all times but compared with Argentina next door, where doves are in plague proportions, here in Brazil, even on newly combined maize stubbles, there were few. There were odd pigeons which looked not unlike a woodpigeon, grey with white wingbars in flight but when perched or on the ground no white bar showed.

When I questioned James tentatively about the prospect of borrowing a gun and a few cartridges he amazed me by saying all bird shooting is illegal in Brazil. It is a serious offence to kill anything. I asked if he meant at this time of year there was a close season. 'No there is a ban all the year.' Not even a 'quackie' for the pot from the lake at dusk? 'No – nada.' (one of the few Portuguese words I learnt.)

So what of other conservation? No dead trees can be felled. The reason for this seems very sound as if locals could cut down dead trees for fuelling their kitchen hearth then live trees would soon become dead trees and the landscape would then have no trees. So how does the Brazilian government resolve the dichotomy of a commendable policy to preserve every tree in this part of southern Brazil contrasting with permitting the devastation of vast tracts of Amazon rainforest in the north. Brazil, from all accounts, is more stable politically than most South American countries so all the more pity such good timber conservation policies cannot apply across the country, especially in the Amazon where it not only creates a national impact but a global one.

Get back in the shade painting under your umbrella Garfit – don't let the sun addle that little brain with controversial conservation politics. Noel Coward was right 'Only mad dogs and Englishmen go out in the midday sun.'

A Caledonian Odyssey

As I travelled north to paint the wonderful land where grouse meets salmon, salmon meets trout, trout meets pigeons and stag meets all, I mused on the controversial question. Why was not the grouse the RSPB emblem? It is after all the only bird that is found in Britain and nowhere else in the world.

I appreciate that birdy books refer to *Lagopus lagopus scoticus* as a subspecies of the willow grouse but it is still a fact that our red grouse is only indigenous to the British Isles. But no, the actual RSPB emblem is the avocet, a splendid bird indeed but it is limited to east coast brackish marshes and then for only a few months of the summer. Hardly a bird the average person, town or country, can in any way connect with as being typically British.

The distribution map of the red grouse shows it to extend over all of Ireland, Scotland, Wales, northern England and down to Devon and Cornwall. I wish that range was still a true picture of this special bird. It is a species now only found in numbers where active keepering is still deployed. Look at the lessons proved by the Langholm report. This conclusively showed more than just the hen harrier predation statistics but the much broader implication of the predator trap for grouse without management once the population drops below a natural sustainable level. This is happening over large areas of Britain where grouse were found a hundred years ago – a long time to man but a mere grain of sand in the hourglass of the species. Not only did the red grouse survive, but with keepering support it thrived and so produced a shootable surplus.

This is a species that is very special but becoming frail over much of its home range. A great opportunity for the RSPB to rise to the challenge. We know why the grouse is not their emblem as people, politics and little old lady legacies are more important than a threatened sporting species. As an optimist I am sensitive to rays of encouragement from the RSPB. Their acknowledgement of the plight of the grey partridge is good news and co-operation with the Game and Wildlife Conservation Trust is to be fully encouraged.

Oh yes, as I was saying before I went into long journey philosophising mode, I was on my way to paint in northern Scotland. My good pigeon shooting friend Andy Hill in Aberdeenshire is retiring to France. I have had so many wonderful times staying with him and his wife Kitty and had planned a last visit to take them both out for a nice meal to thank them for those good times. My plan was hijacked, as when I arrived Kitty had prepared a delicious last supper – almost biblical in significance – but it was more than just bread we shared with a quantity of fine wine. 'No good taking it back to France', said Andy as he opened another bottle. A nostalgic and truly special evening. It was about one o'clock in the morning when Andy said he'd made a hide in a gorse bush beside a pea field for a duty shoot. Would I like to have a go shooting the pigeons in the early morning. Whatever time of day or night I never have a difficulty in saying 'yes' to the prospect of shooting a pigeon.

It was a short night as we set off at 6 a.m. for a 10 mile drive up into the hills. A handful of pigeons flapped off as we arrived and a few young rooks lazily departed. Hardly a field with a buzz, but what a joy to be out. The only gun not sold or packed by Andy was his father's old wildfowling magnum with a broken stock mended by him with glue and a screw, but which had set like a badly healed bone. Full choke in both of its 32" barrels was going to test the hangover.

Andy helped set up before departing to go home and continue packing for the move. He said he'd return about ten o'clock to see how things were going. I sat in solitude in early morning sunshine, pure joy to be out on a surprise whim. This was the country where grouse and pigeon met as the hill farms gave way to moorland and the curlews calling were common to both. Suddenly, I was aware of a pigeon approaching low over the field and felt the connection between pigeon and grouse. Albeit not the same speed and certainly not that of a downwind safety seeking, Exocet, October grouse. However, not all grouse are fast and the humble woodpigeon can match grouse on an upwind drive. This pigeon came on and did just that, offering a low on-coming shot. The heavy magnum found its mark though not in the centre of its choke pattern. It landed with a badly mangled right wing. My eager friend, Conon, also realised this was a bonus shoot as he had watched only the painting gear and an odd smuggled fishing rod being loaded into the back of the car around him. Now he did not need to be told twice to retrieve this wounded bird. With the speed of a greyhound he was out and picked it.

A steady line of pigeons developed from around the shoulder of the distant hill ahead of me having come from forestry away up the glen. I soon got used to the gun but with full chokes closer birds became more difficult and long shots easier. I was therefore, building a bag of silly misses but surprising kills. Odd rooks passed by from time to time and they too joined the ever-growing flock of decoys.

I soon realised that Andy's anticipated fifteen or twenty pigeons was an underestimation. By 9 a.m. I had counted nearly fifty by my clicker. By the time

Andy visited at 10 a.m. I was on eighty. I suggested he take over but he was on the way to Banchory and would come back in an hour.

Still the sport continued to the background piping from curlews and plover. Was it a peregrine I saw on the distant moor? I could not be certain. I hoped Mrs Grouse was not threatened after hatching her brood. I decided that 11 a.m., or the magic hundred, would be my cut-off point of time. It was the latter and by the time Andy reappeared I had been out with Conon to retrieve long outlying dead birds. On borrowed time, and at risk of Kitty's wrath for being late, Andy took over for a couple of hours before his conscience overcame sporting enthusiasm and took him home, having added another thirty to the bag.

I in the meantime was on my way over the Cairngorms to Grantown-on-Spey, Inverness and the A9 north. I arrived as planned at Badanloch, the furthest of the six Helmsdale Lodges. A greeting, a drink and then a recce for the painting, and again the sound of moorland birds. After dinner the party went back to the river and I went for a trout in the loch to soak up the atmosphere. I returned with a basket of vermilion-spotted little brown trout for breakfast; each fought like a tiger for its size. Next morning one of the party was leaving for home, would I like to fish his rod? Am I lucky or am I not? The Helmsdale had not been its normal bountiful self that week and only two fish had been caught by the party. I was sent with Alec the ghillie, a man with eternal enthusiasm and optimism whether fish are being caught or not. For me a rare joy to cast a line on water that salmon could swim. You've got it in one – I am lucky. By 10.15 a.m. Alec had my fish in his landing net. Not the largest salmon, in fact about the smallest grilse. It was the first of the season and only 4½ pounds but it was as special to me as Miss Balantine's record fish from the Tay.

What a sporting twenty-four hours: one hundred pigeons, a basket of trout and a salmon – a mid-summer MacNab perhaps. However, with all that excitement, followed by a successful week's painting and a list of nearly fifty species of birds recorded in the Strath there was not a sight or croak of a grouse. As recently as ten or twelve years ago grouse were like flies along the roadside and in August many days walking-up or shooting over pointers produced wonderful sport. Is this another area where the population has slipped below the predator trap? I hope this is not true and that the future will see their return. However, it is depressing that there, as for many areas of the British Isles, the only grouse now will be found in a bottle!

The Confessions of a Sporting Artist

The day dawned of my first partridge shoot of the season. Excitedly I had prepared everything the night before from coat to cartridges, boots to brown polished cartridge bag, dog whistle, lead and water. In the morning I put my gun and spare gun into their slips, the car was loaded up, Conon hopped in the back and off we went. I had arranged to call on John the mower man to collect my repaired strimmer as I passed him on my way to the shoot.

On arrival we were all bright-eyed and bushy-tailed. It was the exciting first day for most of us and spirits were high. Paraphernalia was decanted from cars to the Guns' bus and dogs milled about with tails a-wagging.

Then it hit me – my gun – my guns, no not in the back of the car – no not on the rear seat – yes, still in their slips on my table in the studio at home. How stupid could I be? I've seen others suffer such amnesia in the past but never me – today it was my turn. I sidled quietly up to my host and in hushed tones told him of my predicament. This was a mistake as a hushed tone of voice is immediately of

interest to others and they heard. My host was quick and kind to suggest a gun from his cabinet but my friends laughed mercilessly as the news spread to all present. My life was not worth living as banter and jokes hailed upon me. 'Rude to your host to assume you would not get a shot worth bringing a gun', 'left it in a pigeon hide yesterday I suppose', 'worn it out' – they loved it. Then one wag saw my strimmer in the back of the car which started a new round of hilarity – 'not very complimentary to the quality of your host's birds if you come with that' or 'is it the weeds on the drive you're trouble-shooting today?' I'll never live it down.

So off we went through corridors, steps, passages, into the depths of the cellar. Ashamedly I followed my host. Bolts, keys, combination locks and eventually we were in the gunroom. He handed me a Holland & Holland belonging to his son. I put it to my shoulder and it seemed to more or less fit, although it was certainly a more valuable weapon than my own at home.

Back up in the light of day and after the delay the boys were refuelled with more banter 'maybe the birds will have a chance today with the artist using another gun.' The first drive produced one partridge over me and I was pleasantly surprised to see it drop to shot as well-trained birds should do. In fact as the day went on the Holland & Holland proved to fit perfectly and I suspect it had fairly tightly choked barrels as, at whatever range, partridges just folded in a tight ball and landed without a twitch.

The injustice of the day then was reversed as I was in the pound seat for the main morning drive. The birds channelled and then came over tall beeches straight to me. I had wonderful sport for about twenty minutes. After that drive the bantering subsided – no jokes – just one wry remark suggesting my host should take the gun away from me.

After lunch more jokes about an afternoon strimming in the orchard, etc. The boys were like terriers with a rat – they just kept shaking it.

The last drive of the day and we were all moved two pegs to our left to account for the wind. You've guessed it – that put me in the pound seat again. Before a drive, it is when you see the pickers-up close in behind you that you suspect you're going to get the shooting. I did. I enjoyed it immensely and a disproportionate percentage of the bag had been accounted for by the borrowed gun. At tea it was suggested I should make an offer for it. Certainly I will not live it down and as those present will spread the story I thought I may really please them by sharing it here now. The moral of the story is don't let it happen to you!

The Crime of Kilsomething Castle

The first week of September has, over the last few years, become special to me as a hallowed pilgrimage to Scotland with my Anglo-American friend Barry to share the joys of sporting camaraderie.

We had enjoyed joining a party for two days driven grouse, followed by two days of rabbits and we were to have a final day pigeon decoying. However, Steve, our guide for the rabbits, had not found anything very promising for our pigeon decoying next day.

As Barry and I travelled to the hotel that evening I saw a stubble field opposite the hotel gates with a number of pigeon feeding and others coming and going – then the

An alert rabbit

farmer appeared in his tractor from the next field. We drove up and introduced ourselves and asked what the position was regarding the pigeon shooting. He was very affable and said it was perfectly all right for us to shoot there the next day and in fact it was the hotel manager who in the past had occasionally been pigeon shooting there. The farmer said he would phone and explain and we could discuss it with the hotel manager that evening. Indeed, the manager was there to greet us and yes, he was pleased for us to shoot as he had not had time for pigeon shooting for months. I then phoned our guide Steve who was delighted we had found a field and would meet us at 9.30 next morning with kit for hides and decoys, etc.

It had all seemed too easy. We settled into the bar at the Kilsomething Castle Hotel, a place with a wonderful yesteryear charm and formality in which even Monsieur Poirot would have felt comfortable. The large high ceilings, oak-panelled rooms and courteous staff created an atmosphere in which one felt that no crime greater than being late for dinner was likely.

Next morning it was raining that steady relentless rain that is the butt of Scottish jokes. However, we met Steve and made a double hide using my angler's umbrella I had in the car from the previous week's painting trip. This being 8 feet across was perfect when covered with camouflage nets and thatched with docks and grasses.

Seated inside, Barry and I were dry and though we could not shoot overhead we had a good arc of fire forward over the decoys.

In spite of the weather the pigeons started to arrive and decoyed well. We took turns as each opportunity of a shot arose. We soon extended the decoy pattern and augmented it with the odd rook and crow which made the mistake of coming within range. It was about half past eleven with all the best feeding time of the afternoon ahead. We had already shot forty or so and were excited about the prospect of a great day.

But no – a Land Rover approached up the field which needed no siren or flashing light, its body language indicated trouble. Two betweeded keepers jumped out. The headkeeper asking with controlled politeness what the hell we were doing. I was out of the hide explaining how we had permission from both the farmer and the man who had the pigeon shooting. To cut a long story short they were placated but should have been informed. They finally agreed that we could continue but they would go and see the Laird of the estate for his jurisdiction.

I suddenly realised as I returned to the hide that my friend Barry who, from dawn to dusk, scarcely draws breath between constant high-pitched chatter and laughter had, for once, fallen silent. Furthermore, it was the first time he had heeded my advice to keep down and not be a jack-in-the-box in a hide. Throughout the whole confrontation he was quiet and hidden on the floor of the hide!

We shot a few more birds then half an hour later back came the keepers – and no, the Laird would not allow us to continue. Oh dear – in 40 years of pigeon shooting, welcomed by farmers from Devon to Inverness-shire, never has the *Shooting Gazette's* pigeon columnist been shown off the field. We packed up wet soggy nets, sacked bedraggled dead birds and phoned Steve to meet us. Then a smart Land Rover appeared and this time it was the Laird himself, not angry or agitated but unhappy about us shooting in the vicinity of two pheasant release pens. He ended kindly saying how pleased he would be for us to shoot pigeons on other stubbles in the future away from that particular area of the estate.

It all goes to show that not only is reconnaissance important, but also to fully inform all involved. At home I always do so but on this occasion, on unknown ground, the misunderstanding was unfortunate. Anyway Steve had found a few pigeon on a field near his home and we made the most of the afternoon there.

We returned to the hotel that evening a little late, like two naughty schoolboys where we were met by the matronly manageress who gave us a 'tut-tut'! Everyone seemed to know of our crime. It did not need Monsieur Poirot to line up all the staff and guests in the lounge – Barry and I were the guilty parties. I looked at the dinner menu and said to the waiter that I was surprised not to see 'Kiljoy Castle Estate Poached Pigeon Served on Grilled Artist' as the main course accompanied by 'American CranBarry Sauce'.

Sport for All Seasons

A reflective moment - The Horseshoe Lake at Hauxton (from a painting by W.G.)

One evening a few years ago my son, Henry, and I were fishing together on the Horseshoe Lake on my small reserve, shoot and fishery near home. It had been one of those rare and special evenings when the trout rose well and took the fly confidently. They fought like marlin in the cool clear water giving wonderful sport.

As we admired the sparkling rainbows and a butter-flanked brownie at the end of the day, we recalled the evening just a few weeks earlier at the end of January when we had stood on the same spot and each shot a duck. I had put my friends in the hides on another nearby lake, which we feed and attract a few mallard for a shot or two at the end of a late season shooting day. A group of five Canadas circled high as we watched and then flew lower over the lake where the guns were still awaiting the last of the duck. A barrage of shots and we were amazed to see four drop and then even more surprised to watch the fifth lone bird turn and fly straight towards us. We fired simultaneously and I could clearly see the double shudder of impact. Its head fell back and it landed with a big splash and was soon retrieved by Conon.

We continued to muse and realised that in little more than an acre we had a full season of sporting recollections. In summer we had so often fished into golden evenings until the swallows had had their fill and the bats arrived for their feast.

Henry learned to swim in the lake as a child and now dives from the fishing platform he helped me build. On hot balmy August days the water is warm enough for me to strip off and go for a swim. Any day of the year suits Conon but he enjoys those swims together when we do synchronised doggy paddle!

On Wednesdays the fishery is closed and in the light evenings Brian, my right-hand man of all things whether keepering, tree production or as bailiff of the fisheries, will come with me and Henry, if he is at home, and enjoy shooting rabbits. They need to be controlled and it makes a good sporting safari with one acting as driver the second as spotter and the third, with silenced .22 rifle, shooting from the vantage point with head and shoulders through the sunroof and a cushion as arm rest on the roof. Usually a sure place for a shot is again on the bank of the Horseshoe Lake.

As summer turns to autumn we have had evenings when my old friend John Humphreys comes with rod and gun. We fish for end-of-season trout but if the geese are heard approaching we lay down the rods, load our guns and kneel in the rushes for a shot. When things go well we return home with both a brace of trout and a goose – fish and fowl make a hearty meal from sport beside the same tuft of sedge. Last autumn, two ospreys, one adult one juvenile, visited on their migration south. They too showed how to catch the end-of-season trout.

Then after all the rods and fishing gear have been hung up for the winter the same stage has a quick change and is set for the last drive of the shooting day. Numbered pegs have been positioned on the outer grass curve of the Horseshoe Lake and Guns await the pheasants which fly across the water having been driven from game crops grown way beyond the lake. Those pheasants see the Guns and climb to top the poplars. These trees were planted soon after I made the lake in 1979. My vision was for them to grow to over 100 feet tall and produce pheasants to test even the most accurate of my friends. Those poplars are already 80 or 90 feet

and the pheasants make very acceptable sport even now. At the same time the duck fly from lake to lake and Guns need to keep looking through 360 degrees, as while pheasants come from the front, the mallard may come from behind.

We do not get the hard winters now but it is the same lake on which the children learned to skate and we will skate again I am sure, if Jack Frost returns one winter and the leather of my old skating boots has not become too hard.

February and March can once again come up sporting trumps as the willows on the corner of the lake are a favourite pigeon roosting spot. Henry had a good flight there and some great shots one January and I went there in early March and tried setting out a dozen decoys on the grass beside the lake, in front of the willows. This worked surprisingly well and attracted other pigeons to fly over the willows where I waited. Conon retrieved from amongst the trees or the lake itself and by dusk we had a good bag.

So all in all, this magic acre produces sport in every season and beauty on every day. As Henry and I made our way back to the hut to weigh our fish we agreed it was our favourite sporting spot in the world.

Neighbourly Relations

A phone call from a local farmer friend about pigeons on his spring rape was to spark off something of a challenge. He had seen a flock of a couple of hundred on his two small fields of spring rape in the nearby parish.

I went to investigate next day and yes, sure enough, there were pigeons – actually more than he had suggested but only then did I see the difficulties involved in trying to shoot them. One field of about 6 acres was behind some houses. The second field was even smaller, only 4½ acres. It was square with one side adjacent to the road and a house on three of its corners. Therefore both fields had two similar problems – firstly, there was no safe arc of fire into either field from any side and secondly, disturbance to the occupants of the houses could be socially difficult. Am I getting more sensitive in my mature years or is it the increasingly delicate political issue of shooting? Probably a little of both but the crop was certainly being decimated in such small fields. I decided to shoot on the Monday to minimise disturbance to those in the village snoozing in their gardens on a Sunday afternoon.

Plan A was to put plastic bags on the 6 acres adjacent to the eight or ten houses to keep off pigeons and hopefully bring them onto the smaller field where I proposed to shoot. I then visited the three adjoining houses and was pleasantly surprised that the chap on the western corner was all for the pigeons being shot to save his vegetables. The little old lady on the north side was equally enthusiastic and urged me to shoot the pheasants too! I explained that was not my remit nor legal at the end of May. Nobody was home at the third house on the southern corner, so I popped a note through the letterbox. So much for local PR and I felt better now that I had support rather than aggro from at least two out of three neighbours.

The next problem was how to shoot safely. Luckily, there was a south-westerly breeze, which meant I could make a hide under the old oak in the field. It was easy to make a good hide so that my decoys were between me and the eastern corner. The boundary of the field was only 35 yards away so any bird between me and the ash tree on that edge was well within range. I could then shoot safely over open fields with the sound of my shots taken on the wind away from the houses and village.

So it was about 2 o'clock when I set up and immediately had one or two customers. I started with just a dozen static decoys but the new dead birds were added to the picture. The other advantage of angling my shots as I did was that the shooting disturbed any pigeons that had come to the 6 acres and trees around it. They immediately flew to my field, not being able to place the bang which had put them on the wing. This meant that when one or two made shots I would nearly always get another shot within a minute. I had to be very careful to keep strictly to my limited arc of safe fire so as not to drop shot anywhere near the houses. This gave only a narrow angle of about 45 degrees. On so many occasions I could have shot birds on my left or right but had to refrain. However, the sport was not just steady but brisk with most birds coming as singles.

The shooting was not particularly difficult as they either decoyed well or made satisfying crossing shots flying along the tree tops at a known 35–40 yards. In such a cosy corner it was possible to shoot very consistently and things were going well. So well in fact that after two hours there were a hundred on my clicker. I had originally thought of taking just a cartridge bag out hoping for forty or maybe fifty birds, but luckily I had taken a case of 250 instead.

There was a lull at about half past four but an hour later with a sunny evening, sport picked up again. The main line came from over my right shoulder passing downwind between me and the field boundary ash tree. Rather than wait for them to pass and maybe turn upwind they made better sport on their first downwind pass. It also meant that those following just saw the leader collapse among the decoys and they came on and in many cases did the same!

Tim, the farmer, came to watch from the road for a while as he heard the steady shooting from the farm. By 6.30 p.m. there was another hundred on the clicker and I was running short of cartridges and half an hour later the last shot fired to end play on 221. Luckily it was a very good moment for Tim to reappear and as he approached his eyes widened – he saw the bad news that half the field was grazed flat by pigeons and the good news that it was covered by a carpet of grey bodies. Crop protection and good sport makes great friends of farmers and pigeon shooters.

We picked most but I was reluctant to let Conon hunt the hedge too much for the last few outliers while game is nesting. Such a good day is rare but never had I shot a bag like that on such a small field. Before driving home I revisited the three neighbours to offer them birds from the day's sport and nature's own bounty.

Truly Glorious

The glorious twelfth – a day of which shooting men love to dream, the press love to scandalise and 'antis' love to spoil. Where will I be? At home with those dreams. However, some of my happiest shooting memories were of seasons in the late 1970s and through the 80s when with chums from Dumfriesshire we used to walk-up grouse at Leadhills.

Like many happy experiences in life one does not fully acknowledge how good they were until they are no more. I do remember just how exciting was the prospect of setting foot on the hallowed heather of the moor – it was Leadhills at its peak. Andrew Duncan from Dumfriesshire was our team leader. He gathered a few local mates and a brother or two to make a team of six Guns. The party changed over the years but the spirit, banter and sport did not. Kenny Wilson was headkeeper in those years, not only a brilliant keeper with a passion for his moor but with great respect for the grouse itself. Indeed he was one of the most charming and interesting men with whom one could be privileged to walk the hill. Also in the subtle grey/blue estate tweed were Tommy, Billy and Willy the underkeepers.

Leadhills is reputedly the highest village in Scotland and the centre of some of the prettiest moorland of south-west Scotland. The steep-sided Lowther Hills were producing exceptional grouse shooting in those days and we had the joy of two to four days from 12 August each year depending on the season. In our late 20s and early 30s we were as fit as greyhounds and like coiled springs as we set off up the hills on the first morning and somewhat less so as we reached the tops. The first covey always seemed to flush at the least expected moment. Sometimes we walked the prime heather of the main drives to wild-up the birds for the first driven days the following week. On other occasions we walked the steep braes which did not come into the main drives. Kenny was brilliant at angling the line for the wind and when we were on a hillside walking upwind he would keep the top Guns well ahead. The grouse they flushed would fly forward, hit the wind and turn to come fast and sometimes very high downwind over the lower Guns, creating testing driven shots.

One afternoon beat was a round hill which the grouse were reluctant to leave and so two Guns were positioned crouched in a hollow in the heather, one about 50 yards further up the hill than the other to intercept the grouse as they flew round the contour of the hill. This became known as the Bhabu Khan beat, as on a warm afternoon Beachie, one of Kirkcudbrightshire's eccentric characters, sported a light cotton safari-type shooting vest he had had made to his own design by some Indian tailor in a back street of Bombay. His name was immortalised for us on that hill.

Andrew's brother, Archie, had somewhat slower reactions than usual one day after customary Dumfriesshire hospitality the night before. A grouse rose in front of him and swung my side and I shot it as another two flushed from the same place. One went left when Arch was looking right and Andrew shot it by which time I had shot the one that went right. Occasionally on warm days a covey of grouse sometimes rose intermittently. So on this occasion as each bird flushed Arch was too slow or was watching the wrong bird. When the last pair flew one went forward which Andrew took while Arch marked but by the time he had turned I had shot the bird behind. Andrew and I had accounted for all eight birds of the covey without Archie firing a shot. His only spontaneous reaction of the event was his shout: 'May the bristles drop out of your brushes, painter.'

On one of our days the estate had arranged a dog trial. Handlers from all over the country were there and also drawn for a run was Billy Steel, the current underkeeper, who was always a bit handy with his dogs but had never entered a trial. Mid-August did not see dogs at the peak of fitness and it was soon evident that Billy's Leadburn Prince was down to the last few. By mid-afternoon his dog was the winner. Billy just handled it as he did every day of the season to retrieve game and do the business. Nothing fancy with whistle or hand signals, just a good honest working relationship between man and dog. So started Billy Steel's rise to fame as one of the top trainers, Leadburn Prince as a great sire and later Billy's son 'Young' Billy too was destined for great trialling accomplishments.

After the trial Kenny Wilson invited all the handlers to join the line of Guns for the rest of the afternoon. We hit a purple patch and it was not just the heather. In little over an hour we shot over forty brace. All the dogs were worked to a standstill – except one, the champion Leadburn Prince who was still up on his toes and the only one fit as we came off the moor.

Oh happy days – with wives joining us for a sumptuous picnic which Andrew's wife Eileen produced from a hamper as we lolled in the heather. Children came too and several of our sons shot their first grouse on those days when the 12th was truly glorious.

SIT DOWN EVENTS OR SANDWICHES – WHICH SHOOT LUNCH IS BEST?

'I know nothing about art but I know what I like', is a comment I frequently hear from those I meet as I sit painting. I find myself saying something similar when face to face with a wine buff and as my culinary skills are limited to eggs, boiled or scrambled on a Sunday evening it is equally appropriate to food.

The happy fact is that I enjoy all shoot lunches, but is that because I love all shoot days? The style of lunches varies as much as the different forms of the sport. The sit-down event in the dining room of the big house is as appropriate as a 'piece' on the hill when walking grouse or stalking. It is a joy to loll in the heather with a venison-filled bap and a beer or dram accompanied by a few chums and the keeper after walking for miles for a few well-earned grouse. Or to be huddled behind a rock as yet another squally shower strikes the high ground where you and the stalker seek shelter. Rain drips off the peak of your cap as you incline your head to take a bite of soggy sarny. When cold and wet my favourite pick-me-up is a cup of black coffee with a spoonful of heather honey and a slug of scotch.

Most of my early experiences were local rough shooting days with farmer friends. Usually we each brought our own packed lunch but on some occasions a picnic feast was provided by the farmer's wife.

Time dictates the scale of set piece driven shooting days. There are let days when lunch is prolonged because the bag is over in the morning so there will only be one drive in the afternoon. Alternatively, there are those extended lunches when the host ensures a full day and one ends the last drive with visible flames from shots fired in the dusk.

I always feel sorry for the hostess when I hear the host on his mobile explaining that we will be late in for lunch. Understandably, all love and sweetness is rarely the response.

So what is the favoured meal? Pheasant casserole or game stew are obvious ideas. The pheasants from the week before are only taken by the game dealer as a favour so why not let the Guns enjoy them. A good joint is always a winner, or beef casserole in one form or another is a good wholesome alternative. Steak and kidney pie is popular and pudding even more so. Talking of puddings, the sweet sort I mean, some hostesses think men don't do puds – but most of us do and love them. We are all schoolboys at heart especially having fun together on a shooting day and simple, solid well cooked food is what seems to touch the spot.

Exceptions to this are the special gourmet events where the shoot is just an excuse for an amazing gastronomic

experience. Such were the days with Archie and Prue Coats at Towerhill. The shoot was a triumph, not only of Archie's keepering but his diplomacy. The 13 acres around his house in Hampshire were all managed for game. Not surprisingly some of the birds from neighbouring estates visited his pheasant heaven and on a shooting day those neighbours were invited to shoot and stood on their own land while their keepers and friends drove their pheasants back over them. After which everyone thanked Archie for a wonderful shoot and came in for Prue's lunch.

Now Prue Coats – you may know from her country cookbooks – is no ordinary lady of the kitchen so the morning's shoot was followed by a full afternoon's lunch. The dining room tables were heaving under so many of the most exquisitely cooked dishes, mostly game and home produce. A choice of pâtés – grouse, trout, smoked pigeon or liver of duck or grouse; terrines of pigeon and mallard; mousses; salads of blended greenery and herbs to accompany oxtail stew, venison or devilled kidneys. These were followed by chocy pots, elderberry mousse or tangerine sorbet; cheeses and coffee. Definitely days on which you did not need to bring your own packed lunch.

Have We Had the Best Shooting?

'We've never had it so good', was the phrase MacMillan famously used to describe the state of the nation in the late 1950s – or was it early 60s? Anyway, as I stood at my peg waiting for a pheasant drive to start, it crossed my mind that it is probably a very true statement now about our sport of shooting.

There are more shoots today than at any period of history, producing more days shooting for more people. There is an opportunity for anybody to get shooting to suit their pocket. Yes, of course, the cream of sport is expensive and the bigger days of high Devon pheasants or driven grouse do cost serious money. However, there are thousands of us who shoot pigeons or rabbits for free. Rough shooting is available at modest cost and DIY farm shoots can produce driven days of amazing value.

Just think of the variety of shooting available in Britain. There are over thirty species of game and wildfowl. Many have their own form of sport as with wildfowling, whether flighting on inland ponds, marsh or foreshore. There are nine species of duck and four of geese that can produce sport. There are woodcock shoots in Cornwall, snipe shoots in Ireland, Devon and the Western Isles. Golden plover can be called or decoyed. Grouse, pheasant and partridge can be walked-up or driven. From wildfowling at sea level, to ptarmigan above the snow line, there is a quarry to challenge and give us sport. Coot, moorhen, feral pigeon, magpie, crow, jackdaw and jay are among the other legal quarry to come to hand on any lowland shoot day. What about the fun walking-up or ferreting rabbits? Hares – blue in the uplands or brown in the lowlands, produce a day's shooting in themselves.

There are more shooting schools and clay clubs with good instructors to help the young or anybody new to the sport. Shooting is well served by a number of organisations working hard for us. We should support them all and everyone who shoots should be a member of BASC and the Countryside Alliance. Everyone involved in game shooting should also support the Game and Wildlife Conservation Trust who have produced the recipe for rearing, releasing and managing game as well as researching the importance of game management for the benefit of all wildlife in the countryside. *The Code for Good Shooting Practice* is an invaluable guide and shows how, in Britain, we take the responsibilities of game shooting seriously.

We contribute greatly to local economies – not just by directly or indirectly employing keepers and beaters, but by use of hotels, pubs and caterers. I'm not advocating drinking while shooting but there are the moments of any shoot day when hospitality and camaraderie are the essence.

To acknowledge everything that is so good now is important but this will not last if we are not careful. There are too many rats gnawing at the foundations of our sport. Erosion of the structure will cause the collapse of so many forms of shooting without any ban as such. The list is growing of threats I fear within ten years. They include further controls on law-abiding gun owners, various forms of vermin control, reduction of quarry species, limits to rearing directly or indirectly through bans on medication, extending the use of non-toxic shot to game shooting and even clay shooting. Other fears include adverse public opinion fuelled by 'antis' and politicians, both British and European, may play unexpected cards to erode our sport.

However, right now we enjoy the greatest era ever of game shooting with the finest quality sport combined with, in the most part, sensible quantities. Today, Britain leads in the way we run our shooting sports and is the envy of the world. We can acknowledge and enjoy it all but must be aware of those who threaten it in the future.

Marauding Friends and Sportsmen

Mallard drake

The last two days of our season at Hauxton Pits are known as Maraud I and II. Although the area of the shoot is only 85 acres we enjoy nine days shooting. Five normal driven days before Christmas, then the Helpers' Day in early January when as two teams we beat and stand at alternative drives before then dispersing to flight pigeons, duck and then geese. By the headlamps of the cars, when all is gathered in, there can be a bag of over a hundred head – the best bag of the season. We then return home for Gina's great shoot supper.

On the seventh day of the season many of the drives are reversed which catch out some of the elusive cocks. So by the time of the Marauds we are chasing the wildest, fittest and cleverest birds of the season. However, they meet their match as eight of us gather at 9 a.m. in the yard.

We all started at Hauxton in our twenties and now nine of the regular fifteen beaters and pickers-up have qualified for the 30-year loyalty bonus: the chance to walk to the point of exhaustion after eleven drives followed by the pigeons, duck and geese flights. As we set off our spirits are high. My friend Brian, who over the years has progressively done more of the keepering, is not known for an abundance of information sharing. However when pushed reluctantly admits with his wry smile, 'We might see one or two'.

Those with dogs inevitably have to do more of the thick woodland drives. Bob Bradford is known as Bob 'the ratman' as he was pest officer for the council. He now has the sixth generation of his spaniels to work at Hauxton. I doubt there is any Kennel Club registration but they work till they drop for Bob. Not only does he breed a good line of spaniels, his own genes are in his strapping son James: not only a good eye with the gun but a brilliant batsman who has scored many boundaries. Now a third generation of Bradfords is seen as James's son Matt is there with great enthusiasm. To complete the Happy Families set Jen and Wendy, Bob and James's wives, also come when they can.

Not all the drives are up to your waist in bramble, rush, reed or water, where spaniels are a must. So the boys with dogs get a stand when we do the maize strips or thin woodland. Bob usually has a pheasant or two to pick. If not then there's a story of the bird he missed, which is worth more to the day than if the bird was in the bag.

After four drives we gather for a draw on our coffee flasks and a chocaholics break as we devour a pack of Penguins or Kit-Kats. Lindsay or John keeps us amused with banter – there always needs to be a joker in the pack on any shoot day.

One year while I was an armed stop on the corner of End Wood a squirrel heard the oncoming beaters and ran up a willow but made the mistake of hiding from them on my side of the trunk. Conon retrieved another various for the bag.

The same year, Reg was delayed as he needed to finish some ploughing before joining the Maraud but soon shot a brace of pheasants which slipped out sideways from the next drive. John also had a good shot there but in spite of all the dogs hunting the marsh we failed to pick it. Back in the cabin, the last of the season's cherry brandy and King's ginger was consumed with our sandwiches. 'Come on – we're not finished yet!' We had done seven drives in the morning and had four in the afternoon. Poor Lindsay, the oldest of us who hung up his gun several years ago, had walked, beating for all the drives. Still the jester, the one-liners kept coming. 'Only one who can still pull the birds', he shouts to Bernie, who emerges with the only pheasant from the last drive. Twenty-nine cocks, seven mallard, fifteen pigeons, two coots, one moorhen, one Canada goose, one jay, a rabbit and a squirrel – fifty-eight head for a very sporting day. Another season produced a record 928 head in the nine days shooting and many happy memories for all involved. Just as on every shoot up and down the land.

On a Glorious First Day of the Pigeon Calendar

I must let you into a secret. At one stage of the previous story of our Maraud on my little shoot, I failed to tell you that I committed the unforgivable sin on a shoot day: I carried my mobile phone. At the end of the afternoon, when we were waiting for a pigeon or two to flight into roost, the phone rang. It was the call I was waiting for with the great news that my younger daughter Penny had given birth to our first grandchild, a little girl, Jemima. As I heard all the details a pigeon flew slowly over me. No – surprise, surprise, I for once did not drop the phone and raise my gun. The easiest pigeon that came in that evening calmly flew on. Such response and restraint must come with the maturity of becoming a grandfather. That evening Jemima was entered in the game book – not under 'various' but in a new column 'births'.

A week later saw grandfather Garfit set off with a car full of kit for the first day's decoying of the season. In spite of a sense of age being forced upon him his youthful enthusiasm was as strong as ever at the prospect of a day out pigeon shooting.

I went to check out an estate I know well where pigeon move in at this time of year to feed on beet tops, chopped game strips or spring drilling. I drove all round and yes there were pigeon about but none of the maize strips had been chopped yet. This work was to start in the next day or two. On the day I visited, ploughing had started on the light land and the drill followed immediately with spring barley. This with the chopped maize strips nearby could look promising for the end of the week.

As it happened this work and parsnip harvesting on another field kept the pigeons on the move. They drifted to trees in an old marl pit in the centre of a field which had a 2-acre block of maize adjacent. For years I had felt there would be a shoot there one day but it had never happened. That day looked possible and I decided to set up, which was easily done with a simple hide on the downwind side of the pit, with the pigeon magnet whirling two dead birds enticingly above the uncut maize. Static decoys would not show well in the standing crop but it was a classic opportunity for the magnet to produce movement and attract passing pigeons. It did. In the bright sun and light breeze they decoyed well. The shooting was not easy though as, although dead pigeons on the magnet attracted their live friends, they dived and twisted, not sure whether to join the feeding party or swoop into the trees behind me. However great sport ensued with the birds coming either singly or in small groups. I had started at 11.30 a.m. and had shot nearly fifty by 1 p.m. when I set about my sandwiches. However, it was a busy half

hour and I would no sooner get a mouthful than I would have to drop the gnawed sandwich and focus on the next incoming bird.

The day had all the dreamlike qualities of a good day's decoying; wonderful fine weather with the woodpigeons looking handsome against a blue sky as they used the wind. Conon, my golden retriever, was behind me watching my every move and retrieving the odd flapper from the the pit when bidden. I've never had such a demonstratively happy dog with his tail wagging all day.

With a hundred on my clicker by 2 p.m. the activity suddenly slowed down and I packed up at 3 p.m. having shot another twenty. After Conon and I had quartered the maize, having collected seven droppers on the edge of the nearby wood, we loaded the car. I called on Bill the keeper and gave him a bottle of scotch with my thanks so he too could enjoy and share the pleasure of my day.

Time Flies

May is not the most exciting month in the shooter's diary but as spring turns to summer it is the time when everywhere is alive with birdsong. It is just so exhilarating to marvel at the extraordinary variety of birds around us, not just our residents looking their smartest in breeding plumage, but the summer migrants too.

For the last year or two I have been more positive in appreciating this special month by inviting a friend or two to spend a day around our cottage in north Norfolk looking for birds. A few years ago John Humphreys, an old shooting mate, had just written an article on the number of birds he had recorded in his garden which prompted me to ask him to join me at Cley. We set off as 'twitchers' for a day: 7 p.m. one evening till 7 p.m. the following day. That was the time we left his house and he had an old RSPB spotter's guide as a checklist. The two-hour

North Norfolk Coastal Marsh (from an oil painting by W.G.)

journey had us covering a number of common species including chaffinch, starling, woodpigeon, kestrel, moorhen, red-legged partridge – a handsome cock on the edge of a field of spring barley – house martin, swallow, blackbird, jackdaw, rook, and carrion crow but no grey partridge on our route.

We arrived at dusk and I drove straight to Salthouse heath for what I hoped might be a treat. Sure enough, clear and melodious was the song of the nightingale. A tawny owl then called from a wood and lapwings were raucously pee-witting out on the marsh. Were we too early for the nightjars which can be seen here in June? No sooner did I suggest it than the hunting call 'go-eek, go-eek' came from the gloaming over the gorse. Such a good start merited a pint at the Dun Cow.

At 4.30 a.m. we were out along deserted lanes where the world was alive with so many birds – willow warbler, greenfinch, yellow hammer, wren, blackcap, blue and great tit – and we also had the joy of coming eyeball to eyeball with our nightingale of the previous evening singing right by the roadside. Down on the marsh the sounds were deafening as we recorded greylag and Canada geese, shelduck, wigeon, mallard, gadwall and teal. Then an inspiring sight as a hobby came over the reed-bed, where we had heard bearded tits.

Everywhere sedge and reed warblers chittered. A marsh harrier quartered the distant reeds often mobbed by lapwings when it came into their nesting territory. Out on the scrapes were the many avocets for which Cley reserve is known, as well as black-tailed godwits, redshank, common sandpiper, oystercatchers, ringed plovers, dunlin, ruffs and reeves as well as a great number of black-headed gulls and common terns, nesting on the islands. Cormorants stood drying out like Batman with extended wings. On the marsh grazing were parties of woodpigeon, Brent geese, the odd heron and a pair of Egyptian geese. Then as a kestrel hovered above, a sparrowhawk patrolled, hunting high along the reed bed.

Back at the cottage we sat with full plates of bacon and eggs outside in the garden overlooking the marsh but every mouthful was disturbed by another species spotted: house sparrow, dunnock, linnet, song thrush, robin, pied wagtail, swift, cuckoo, collared dove and chiffchaff – and all before the last sip of coffee.

Then we met Bernard Bishop, warden of the marsh and an old boyhood friend, and spent an hour in one of the hides. We added pintail, garganey, shoveler and

tufted duck as well as some more obvious species like coot, curlew and the little grebe which popped up in the carrier right in front of the hide.

A ride along the coast taking in more habitat produced goldfinch, wheatear, meadow pipit, skylark, stock dove and the great egg thief – the magpie, but still no sight of the grey partridge. A buzzard circled on the thermals above Holkham woods and the short scratchy phrase of a whitethroat came from a bush when we stopped to have a pee behind a hedge.

From the cliff tops above Hunstanton we saw fulmars, little gulls and sandmartins, and bobbing on the sea a small raft of eider duck resting on their migration north.

As we ate our sandwiches sitting in the marram grass near the beach we saw turnstones and sanderlings running along the shore, and then a party of knot shot past in formation. In the warmth of the sun we lay back in the sand dunes and dozed off. After forty or was it fifty winks – I wasn't counting – we scanned again with binoculars and there on the lagoon behind us was a snipe and surprisingly, a little egret. These white birds with plumes seemed out of place here in Norfolk.

Titchwell, or as some call it Twitchwell, is a remarkable tribute to the best of the RSPB's new reserves with its single path passing through so many different habitats. By now we had covered many of the likely species so it was a joy to find some rarer excitements including black-winged stilt, grey plover, bar-tailed godwit, whimbrel, spotted redshank, little tern and a great thrill for me to hear a cetti's warbler in the distance. However John did not hear it or believe me so we could not count it. Walking back we saw a pair of ruddy duck – where else would you expect to see this banished species than on a RSPB reserve?

As we returned to Cley something made me turn down the beach road and in the evening light as herring gulls returned to roost and reed buntings sat on a dead elder bush, there at last feeding on the marsh were a pair of the hallowed grey partridges.

A cup of tea back at the cottage before heading for home and still more treasures. A short-eared owl hunted over the marsh below and then across our noses in the garden flitted a spotted flycatcher – the first seen of the year.

What a day: one does not have to shoot a hundred pigeons for a red letter day – for us just over a hundred species of birds was as exciting.

The Psychology of Stance and Style

The other day I met Michael Yardley who writes and speaks so well to the media and is an excellent envoy for all shooting sports. I also greatly admire his books, which are some of the most comprehensive on shooting that I have ever read, covering every shooting style and technique. He has chapters on shooters' vision, exercises and, most interesting of all, on the psychology of shooting. Conversation soon turned to our mutual admiration of the legendary Percy Stanbury who won forty-seven championships between 1926 and 1953 in disciplines as diverse as skeet, sporting and down the line.

For many years he was the head instructor at the West London Shooting School where his technique is still taught today. In the early 1970s I had the privilege of meeting and having lessons with the great man and it was the style and elegance of his footwork, balance and timing that epitomised a technique which made me realise shooting was not just an action but an art. This is where Mike Yardley and I soon bonded as fans of the great man.

We arranged to meet, chat about shooting style and analyse Stanbury and others who had influenced our own shooting techniques.

On the appointed day we arrived at the Braintree Shooting Ground near his home in Essex. I had my Beesley which is not so different from the Percy Stanbury heavy, long barrelled side-by-side. Mike had a fine Webley Scott of 1897 again with 30" barrels – not dissimilar to Percy's later model. Interestingly over our shooting lives we have both evolved to using heavier, longer barrelled guns with higher combs.

Out on the ground we started on a straightforward skeet low house target to illustrate and discuss all shooting techniques from Stanbury to Churchill, CPSA to John Bidwell's move, mount, shoot, maintained lead and even the ambush. We both naturally took up the Stanbury foot and body positions, with the body at 45 degrees to the place you plan to take the shot, our feet at 1 and 3 o'clock. Weight on front i.e. left foot. Having set ourselves up for the shot we would pivot back right-handed to address the clay at a point just ahead of where it would first be seen clearly.

As the target appears the body reacts and unwinds back to the forward position where the shot is to be taken. The muzzles of the gun in the Stanbury method start on the line of the target and stay there as the right hand raises the stock, the left hand pushes out, and the shoulder and gun all come together, at which moment, having swung through the line from behind, the gun is fired and the swing continues to follow through. The beauty of this technique is that the body moves gracefully from the feet up through all the joints in rhythm.

How to achieve consistency is something well explained in Mike's book, *Positive*

Shooting. It is the key to all methods based on a triangle of which the three sides must equally interrelate: 'visual contact', 'balance' and 'rhythm'. The first is application of eye and mind, the second is the body and the third is the co-ordination of timing throughout the three parts of a shot: whether it is 'bum, belly, beak; move, mount, shoot, or 'you are dead'. Michael's style demonstrated a very even sense of this rhythm. Mine less so as for pigeon shooting I have developed a technique of watching for the moment of killability and then my up-two-three becomes a fast, single movement – at times too hurried for clays.

THE UNFORGETTABLE FIRST GROUSE

We can all recall with happiness, joy and pride the first bird of any species we shoot. In my early twenties I visited my cousin Timmy Douglas, a wild young farmer who lived up in the Cheviot Hills and farmed sheep on a hill farm. The 'in-bye' paddocks around the house gave way to white ground before rising to open moorland which stretched south across the Cheviots as far as the eye could see to the English border. Somewhere in those thousands of acres of heather there were reputed to be a few grouse.

Timmy's neighbour had the shooting tenancy and occasionally walked up grouse with a few chums. I got permission to do so myself and wished for good luck as grouse were scarce that season. So one afternoon I set off with my trusty 12 bore; game bag over my shoulder and optimism. I had never seen a grouse, let alone shot at one. Hills when young and fit are merely an inconvenience – certainly no obstacle – and I just loved the open space. Cousin Timmy did not shoot and so it was on my own that my eyes and ears took in the sights and sounds of this form of landscape new to the southerner from East Anglia. Wheatears and meadow pipits were rarely found at home but here they were common, as were sounds of the curlew and raven. I flushed a covey of grey partridges which flourish on the white ground but would not be in season until the following month. Then on up into the first heather. Fingers of it stretched down the hill where grass and moorland met on outlying islands, tough and tussocky with edges grazed. Ahead lay the carpet of purple that I had dreamed of seeing. The solitude was immense, the space eternal and the sense of being so alive and yet so small as when gazing at the sky on a clear night was exhilarating.

Where in all this heather were grouse? At home one would hunt a hedge for a pheasant, a stream or pond for a duck but here there were no features to indicate where a covey might be found.

I walked on following sheep tracks

After a number of discussions on a variety of interesting targets we asked ourselves 'what if Percy Stanbury had been shooting with us?' Would he have agreed with our interpretation of his style? Would he have actually adapted his style for some shots? We decided that he would have generally approved but in some cases he would not have held his muzzles as high as the actual line for skeet shots. For fast targets he would not have had time to come from behind but would have assessed this as he mounted his gun to the target with his natural swing.

which criss-crossed the landscape. Suddenly ahead I saw a head appear like a periscope above the heather tops. Then it disappeared and a moment later I saw what had to be a grouse running ahead of me on the sheep track. I then saw another, there were two grouse but no others – no covey but a barren pair. As I quickened my pace so did they. For 20 yards we were in convoy. After another 20 yards I was gaining and they were in shot but they ran on. Were these birds not supposed to be the ultimate sporting challenge as they flew so fast, skimming the heather and changing flight by the slightest twist of a wing? No, this pair just trotted on ahead and then just as I was lulled by their lacklustre performance they exploded into the air and caused me surprise by their sprint for freedom away from this novice on the moor.

However I raised my gun and in one movement sponsored by youthful adrenaline took my shot at the first bird which caught my eye. This was the nearer one following its leader which was 10 yards ahead. I was excited at the prospect of a grouse and so I was keen to make the most of this opportunity – bang! Yes my bird fell but so too did its mate, the leader. Their line had crossed as I fired and so the one shot had not only killed my first grouse but my first brace. What a prize! What a thrill as I smoothed the feathers of each. As I stroked back the eyelid of the cock the red blaze appeared above his eye and his white feather spats covered not only his legs but also his feet like no other bird I had ever seen, except some rare breeds of bantam. Not the most challenging of shots at grouse but I have since experienced their cousins, driven in the teeth of an October gale when one's eyes water as wind and snow cut the air and the grouse are in their element. Man can marvel but stands mocked at the end of a drive. However as I returned off the hill with that first brace I was as fulfilled as any hunter-gatherer of ancient times.

Making the Most of an Unexpected Opportunity

There have been days out pigeon shooting when I have packed up early for lack of action but never had I done so because it was too good. However one day it happened, not just for one reason but two.

When on the north Norfolk coast with my wife, it is a time of holiday and an opportunity to paint the landscape we love. However I always have my gun should I see a few pigeons and the chance of a shoot. I saw pigeon flighting to some laid barley only three fields away from the house. Bernard keepers the farm part-time and we often enjoy a day's pigeon shooting together. However he was away on a fortnight's holiday and had encouraged me to have a go if there was a chance.

I arrived at about half-past one and was surprised to see a good number of pigeons already on the field. I had quite a walk along the headland to get to the place in the hedgerow I felt would best cover the field, with an area of laid barley within range on which to show my decoys. As I settled in to an easily erected hide, my trigger finger was beginning to twitch.

Shooting started immediately as birds came downwind from behind but then saw the decoys and turned to come in. The sound of my shots disturbed a wood half a mile away and pigeons came on upwind, others came from woodland to my right. In fact the only point of the compass pigeon did not come from was the North Sea out to my left.

The pigeon decoyed well and the shooting was fast and furious. Not the most testing, but it is important not to lose focus as any pigeon can change angle so quickly in the air. However, I was on form and had forty-eight birds down for the first two boxes of cartridges. Thinking about Richard Faulds' training for the Olympics got me going and after an hour and a half I had a hundred with only five missed.

The next hour was even more exciting and I had another hundred on my clicker by 4.15 p.m. and wonderful sport taking on all comers – whether downwinders from behind, long crossers or high overhead – and a very long crow.

Sadly my Olympic bid was over as I had taken 108 shots for that second hundred. I'm sure Faulds would not have dropped a shot at all. It was in the second hour that my dilemma, in fact double dilemma, surfaced. Firstly my dear old dog Conon was watching with wagging tail but picking up was going to be difficult.

Secondly if I stopped with still more than three hours of feeding time for the birds, this field would hopefully shoot again when Bernard was home in a week's time. For two good reasons therefore I decided to stop shooting, a difficult decision as I might have easily beaten my own previous record. However I could not ask more of Conon or spoil a chance for Bernard.

I picked all I could see by hand and then Conon worked like a champion. I watered him and let him rest at intervals as I carried sack after sack of birds back to the car. Then with the heart of a lion he hunted again. Barley is not kind to dogs and I would check every ten minutes or so that there were no barley awns trying to work their way into his nose or ears. What a great day.

So what happened the following week? Bernard arrived bronzed from the southern sun and was interested to hear my story. He chided me for not going for my record and giving up, but equally was excited to have a go on such a hot field. We went two days later and struggled to get thirty between us. The birds had departed and split up all over the county to feed. Oh dear – but despite Bernard's recriminations for not shooting on while the pigeon were there I still could not have asked more of my friend Conon, even though he always encourages me to keep shooting too. There is a moral to the story – I'm working on it.

Big Birthday, Big Shoot, Big Trouble

Yes it was the 'big 60' and a weekend of very happy celebrations with family and a few of my oldest mates. There were kind presents to remind me of my age, of items that had worn out after years of good service – like cartridge belt, game bag and shooting coat.

I had a great day's partridge shooting on the day itself in Norfolk but decided a day out decoying pigeon would just complete the celebrations. I had been watching several fields of wheat stubble which, having been subsoiled, had rekindled the interest of a good number of pigeons. It is a difficult area to shoot being on the outskirts of Cambridge and criss-crossed with footpaths, and cycle ways, the main rail line to London and urbanisation on two sides.

On the day it was clear that the fields nearest the town were of most interest and there was a belt of trees which ended in the middle of three stubbles. This would be the place to best cover the situation. The problem was that the wind was a fairly strong south-easterly and if I set up with my back to it my shooting would disturb the community. So I shot with the wind in my face to shoot away from the houses and hopefully smother the sound of my shots. Therefore it was all wrong according to the classic decoying scenario. It started slowly with a few passing shots and I went out from the hide to set up the first ten dead birds. I then had birds start to come out from the suburbs on a line from my left. Some came over the trees and others skewered awkwardly into the decoys as the wind prevented a frontal approach.

I had started shooting at 10.15 a.m. and after only once coming out of the hide the sport just got better and better until I had a hundred by 11.50 a.m. As the wind strengthened it became clear that the birds could not place the sound of the shots and they came in, or over, from all directions. I was having every type of shot in the book as they approached high from my left or like downwind grouse from my right. I had never had such fast action and in the next hour I had another 128 on my clicker and then a similar number in the next hour – over 250 between 11.50 a.m. and 1.50 p.m. which works out at one every twenty-eight seconds. I had taken out two cases of Gamebore clear pigeon cartridges, many more than I have ever fired in a day before, but I realised I was going to run out. I phoned the farm office but the owner was out and the farm manager had no access to cartridges.

I had 390 on the clicker at about 2.30 p.m. when, from the north, the police helicopter appeared. It often does if there is a man on the run or traffic problems.

However it then hovered for a few minutes before starting a wide circle. Actually it did a great job of moving pigeon off two other fields and I kept shooting, but I then had the realisation that I was the centre of its ever-decreasing circles. I was within waving distance to the look out-officer.

Still pigeon came and I was now over the four hundred and the chaps looking down would have seen me in the middle of an acre of grey bodies.

'Hello there, hello there – police approaching', was the cry I then heard from behind. Out of the trees came a figure who was not just a sergeant, but an officer, with a lot of shiny bits all over him. He turned out to be the Cambridge Constabulary Chief Inspector. Was I a criminal? No – I was a law-abiding member of the community pigeon shooting – so I had no reason to feel guilty. I stood up and made a show of unloading my gun before putting it down. From my car they had checked my name with the licensing authorities. Actually it was all very friendly and after a brief assessment of me and my purpose there, the helicopter was told to stand down. I showed a photocopy of my shotgun certificate which I always carry in case of just such a drama. This had already been checked with the firearms department. In fact the Chief Inspector used to enjoy a bit of pigeon shooting himself and was more interested in my sport than the problem. However some well-meaning member of the public had reported a World War Two sound of battle and the police chose to respond purposely. Aerial surveillance was backed up by the local school being put under curfew, with nobody allowed out of the buildings until the ground patrol had assessed the situation. Having clearly seen that I had considered safety and made efforts to minimise disturbance we chatted for nearly half an hour. I suggested that the officers could watch if they removed their yellow vests which did not complement my camouflaged position. However they decided to go and I shot out the last of my two boxes of cartridges by 3.15 p.m. with 437 on my counter. I then took two hours picking up but could not gather birds from the gardens the other side of the field or the belt of trees along the main road where several had collapsed. However I picked over 90 per cent. What an exciting birthday with by far my record day. Maybe there's still life in the old dog yet – if I stay out of prison.

I later contacted the Chief Inspector to discuss a policy to avoid a similar incident in the future. It was agreed that it was impractical for pigeon shooters to notify the police whenever they were in action, although people lamping foxes at night are recommended to do so. However, I have arranged that I will telephone when I am to shoot in that sensitive area in the future or near other residential areas. We countrymen with legally held shotguns are living in an evermore sensitive era created by criminals or lunatics with illegal firearms. Sadly those fields will never produce a good day's sport again. As I write a new road and a thousand houses are being built there. The fields may have gone but nobody can take away that memory.

Singing and Shooting in the Rain

It was our second shoot of the season at Hauxton Pits, my mini shoot, and the day was grey. Not just dull but a persistent drizzle that one did not notice until one was soaked. However, as I drove round early before anyone arrived, the pheasants were busy feeding and looking quite perky. It had not been raining all night and they appeared surprisingly dry.

The Lodge Lake in Summer (from an oil painting by W.G.)

As the beaters and friends arrived spirits were high and banter commenced as soon as the door of each truck opened. Guns arrived too, also full of optimism and joy in spite of the weather. All jumped out of their cars and pulled on wet-weather gear with total disregard for the rain.

Among the friends there that day were three of my *Shooting Gazette* 'dream team': Nick Fane with his jewel of a wife Tal; Barry Littlewood my great shooting mate from America who has been featured in some of my stories (do you remember we were thrown off an estate in Scotland for poaching pigeons?) and his lovely wife Faye was with him, a girl who's always cheerful, in spite of being married to Barry; then there was Richard Faulds, my gold medal hero of the Sydney Olympics and it was great to meet Tanya who was with him. She is pretty, elegant and charming and quite at home in wet weather gear.

I greeted them all and gave the instructions for the day – 'Cocks only, five ducks or seven shots whichever comes first, and shoot what gives you pleasure except the beaters or me.'

I never fix the draw but on this day I did tweak it to get Barry wound up. When he and I were shooting with Nick in Hampshire recently we were placed next to each other on one drive. Nick always places the Guns and knew that on this particular drive we would be in the hot seats and not far apart. Sure enough, we were on the receiving end of a maize strip from which partridges and pheasants came steadily for some time. Now Barry had behaved well when stood next to a Gun he did not know but when next to me he immediately sprouted twisted horns as the Devil in him became uncontrollable. He shot his own birds well but my birds better. The more he leaned across, the more he jumped up and down shrieking with joy as another landed at my feet. I did get a shot or two when he was unloaded or a bird was far to my left. It could have become competitive but I was happy that he was enjoying himself at my expense. He is a very generous host and on his shoot I have been known to put my share in the bag on several days of the season.

So at Hauxton I devised a little scheme for his day. I explained to the friends shooting that I had a Gun who was safe but inexperienced. I said that he wanted me to arrange for a good shot either side to fire at his birds, ideally simultaneously with him so he could claim to have shot something. I therefore asked Nick Fane, possibly the best shot I know, and our Olympic champion Richard Faulds to take the numbers either side of the novice. It was then that Barry tumbled to the fact that it was he who was the filling in the sandwich. The fun started as he begged me for forgiveness and asked his neighbours to let him have a shot. Luckily I know Barry is a good enough shot to hold his own. In fact it was quite a strong team of Guns anyway.

It was on the two afternoon drives where the Guns were more in the open beside the lakes that Barry found his neighbours could help him out. In fact when I appeared at the end of the drive when some mallard had flown over there were a number floating dead in the water in front of Barry. He said only one was his. In fact he had got somewhat twitchy by then and though he had been shooting so well elsewhere he did have a few chinks in his accuracy that day. It could have been because he was too busy laughing! By the last drive Richard had handed his gun to Tanya who proved to be as good a shot as him, which added insult to injury as she wiped Barry's eye a time or two.

All the friends beating were loving it and I can not remember a day with such high spirits throughout. Nobody had noticed that it rained ever harder during the whole day.

Hosting a Field Trial is a Nerve-racking Business

Dog trials are usually run on grand estates or large shoots. Hauxton Pits is neither but when asked to host such an event, it appealed to me as a challenge on the 80-acre shoot. This came about as Doug and Robin Wise are very old friends and Robin has helped picking up at Hauxton for thirty years. As every bird falls in the cover of woodland, bramble, rush or reed, and others splash down on the water, it is a haven for good working dogs. Now it just happens that Robin is also the chairman of the Labrador Retriever Club and so it was she who suggested a trial at Hauxton, as she enjoys working her own dogs there.

So it came to pass that on 20 December our fifth shoot of the season was to be an all-aged stake for twelve dogs. These were to be put under the sharp eye of four judges. Robin had gathered mutual friends: Tess Lawrence, Alan Thornton, Sarah Gadd and Doug, her husband. So it was all a good party with Terry and Gaynor Bailey officiating. One soon realised that, with so many people involved, it was not a normal shooting day and it soon became obvious that it was more a trial for the host than the dogs.

The first drive was from willow woodland, driven over the Guns to drop birds into thick grass, scrub and bramble. Only a few cocks produced retrieves as intended. The first dog to be sent for a bird produced a blank and so the handler was out. I said he was welcome to stay and help Robin as she was the official picker-up of the day.

He was later deployed and while Robin went to hunt the ditch he was to start again from the fall. This he did and his dog immediately picked the bird, dead, under a bramble four yards from the fall. Poor chap had his own dog eye-wipe itself.

The second drive was one of our most reliable, a banker for a dozen retrieves to test the dogs. But no, apparently the noise of the first drive and the shouts and whistles had caused the birds to fly out. So my hot-shot Guns chosen for the day, John Humphreys and his son Peter, Peter Theobald, ace pigeon shot, and Bernard Bishop had but a single hen to shoot for a retrieve. The third drive was a thick area of wet woodland we call the Everglades, and the pheasants there were reluctant to fly forward and skirted out sideways.

It was not just the pheasants that were getting twitchy by now – me too! I decided to invoke plan B. With little to retrieve so far, we had time to do the middle wood as an extra drive. This, thankfully, did produce a show of birds and John shot a woodcock to add variety. The church drive also gave more action but by the time we stopped for soup and a break the dogs had worked and handled beautifully with no more eliminations.

Around the lakes a mallard produced a good test and although it fell dead in open water where there was a crust of ice around the fringe, Mr Oliver's dog, Storm, did good work as he valiantly tried to break the ice but then used its brain and ran around the lake to swim in from the other bank, which was clear of ice. All were impressed and clapped.

The last drive had been planned as a classic test for the finalists. On the Horseshoe Lake the dogs with handlers were on the point of the peninsular, the pheasants driven over them and shot by the Guns on the far side. The dogs were then to swim the 50 yards across and retrieve the dead birds from the willow carr behind the guns. However there were still six dogs in at this stage and at least

CONON HAS A RARE RUN-IN WITH TETANUS

It was the peak of the shooting season at the turn of the year when I became aware of odd changes in the appearance of my shooting partner Conon. His tenth birthday had been in December and apart from the odd twinge and stiffness at the end of a working day, he was a lean, fit boy and a golden retriever in his prime.

However he seemed to age years in the following week. His eyes narrowed and had a rather vacant look, his face went lopsided and most strange was that his ears stood up before turning over at the end like those of a terrier. Now I've got nothing against terriers, but goldens have soft, floppy ears which even when alert do not stand up like those of a Jack Russell that's seen a rat. His coat lacked lustre and he spent less time grooming than usual. Also his tail developed a kink where he had damaged it as a young dog when he went head over heels chasing a

runner as it stopped suddenly at the moment he was about to catch it.

The odd thing was that he was still so perky and full of his normal enthusiasm for a day's sport. There was no reluctance to bounce out of the car on arriving at a shoot. I began to think he had suffered a stroke. I watched him carefully for another day or two. However despite working hard on the Thursday, I decided to take him to the vet the next morning.

Paul and Tina Davey run a very good surgery in Whittlesford, a village just south of Cambridge. The young Italian lady, Angela, was on duty and she was soon looking very serious as she examined my pal. 'This could be tetanus', she pronounced. It is rare in dogs and few cases have been recorded in the practice but she was very positive about her diagnosis. She explained that there was no blood test for tetanus but she would like another dozen birds required to get a result. Would there be birds in the drive today after the general disturbance and things not going to plan?

Thankfully a steady flow of pheasants climbed high but the Guns raised their game to match the quality and fifteen good pheasants and another mallard were more than enough to seal the bid of the winner. By the time everything was completed the prize-giving was in the gloaming. Photographs of the worthy winner, Keith Willimot, were accompanied by flashes as cameras momentarily lit the scene.

There had been excellent dog work and spirits were high as congratulations were spread as evenly as thanks all round. I was much relieved, as although I believe we have enough birds for the rest of the season, they made themselves scarce that day. However the suspense was part of the excitement and thankfully it ended perfectly.

to do tests immediately to eliminate other possibilities, which could be identified in the blood. I agreed to return that afternoon to discuss the prognosis.

It was not good when I saw Conon later that day. He by then did look ill: listless, tired and with a temperature. The blood tests proved clear of any other disease as suspected by Angela. He should stay in and immediately be put on an intravenous antibiotic to zap the bacteria and a tetanus anti-toxin drug. If he did not respond the future was not good. I left him and drove sadly home as a tear rolled down my cheek. I practice Reiki and that evening sent him deep heartfelt, healing energy.

I phoned at midday; there was no change but I could phone again on Monday at noon. On the dot of 12 o'clock I dialled. 'Yes - he's made a remarkable recovery: you can pick him up this afternoon'; said the veterinary nurse. I could not believe it. I was there at 4 p.m. with my arms around him as if welcoming back the prodigal son who was thought to be lost.

Rachel was the vet on duty that afternoon and she had experience of tetanus on three occasions with a pack of foxhounds. She explained that the tetanus bacterium created toxins which circulate in the blood and latch onto the nerves at the spinal cord. Muscle paralysis then sets in causing stiffness – hence the colloquial name of 'lockjaw'. Luckily in Conon's case it was caught in time. After a fortnight's rest while completing the course of antibiotic pills, he made a full recovery and seemed his old self, lively as a cricket and actually very disappointed to be left in the studio whilst convalescing. His features returned to normal during the next week. He has ended the season in good style, his last retrieve being an old Canada goose which he brought from the lake and carried up the bank as if it were no heavier than a teal. A joyous sight for me, and if I had a tail it, too, would have been wagging as happily as his.

Discovering Gold and Silver in Argentina

As a painter of sporting rivers I spend much of my summer enjoying the challenge of capturing their beauty on canvas: a fishing trip for sport alone is very rare. However my good friends Nick and Tal Fane invited me to join them as their guest to the ultimate sporting trip, fishing for wild trout in Patagonia, followed by dove shooting in Cordoba.

In mid-February, and after a long flight to San Paulo in Brazil, we travelled via Buenos Aires to our destination in northern Patagonia, within sight of the snow-capped Andes mountains. It was at the end of their summer and the surrounding hills and plains had an arid Mediterranean appearance. However, the lodge at Tipiliuke where we stayed was like an oasis in the desert – a garden like Eden with a beauty formed by exotic flowers I did not recognise, but so many fine trees of species we have in Europe, all introduced by the pioneering family who developed the estancia for sheep and cattle over the past hundred years.

The climate was like heaven – warm as our finest summer day with clear blue sky. We were just four in the fishing party: Nick and Tal Fane, Josephine, Tal's greatest friend since childhood and me.

Kevin and Mary Jo were the couple who hosted the lodge, in a way that welcomed us as if we were old personal friends. The atmosphere was so relaxed with their kindness and caring that within a short time, I had honestly lost track of all things external and could not tell you the day of the week.

So, having donned waders and sunblock, Nick and Tal would set off with their guide Lucas while Jo and I bundled into Adrian's Toyota twin-cab pick-up truck. After little more than a mile or so bumping along the dusty road we'd turn off through tall mesh gates set in fencing as high as a Scottish deer fence. The cattle were Herefords and Angus, again a familiar sight. Odd llama-type animals lived on the parched vegetation while raptors soared overhead – vultures, hawks and eagles on the thermals with falcons darting and stooping. They were flying in numbers that even the RSPB would have to accept were a threat to the well-being of other bird species.

Then we would come to the willow-banked Rio Chimehuin. A river like a breath of fresh air in the burnt late-summer landscape. It's fast-flowing water so pure that the sparkling sunlight danced in the current, causing the stones on the riverbed to appear as jewels around our feet as we waded. The wild trout were totally camouflaged, and yet a rainbow leaping was a bar of pure silver and a brown trout in the hand an ingot of gold.

Adrian, our guide, was a handsome, bronzed, ex-professional footballer who has a passion for fishing and now lives on the river with fishermen every day. He was kind but positive in his instruction, help and expectation. We fished different beats

each session and he would split his time between Jo and me as we fished different parts of the wide river or adjacent pools on the rivulets. Jo's enthusiasm needed no encouragement as she elegantly cast to cover the next rise, or fish the water below the shady willows on the far bank. Her new rod, a special present, was beautifully light and with a soft action that gave her line a full rhythmical pattern in the air.

Various techniques were favoured on these special fish, which took odd butterflies, bugs or nymphs by day. Both rainbows and brown would rise with great speed and vigour in the fast current to take the fly and require a very spontaneous strike. Whatever the size the one thing every trout had in common was an amazing strength. Their power was to be admired, and these fish of Olympic fitness tested our lines and bent our rods and then every trout was returned to the water with our blessing. All fish were measured in inches rather than by weight and a fish of 18 or 19 inches was a big one – however Josephine caught a monster, which did qualify to be referred to by weight. Adrian estimated it was 6½ or 7 pounds. I never saw her great fish. However the smile on Jo's face and the glow of joy as she told the story later, of her largest ever trout, was enough.

The climax of each day was the evening rise, when for a mere quarter of an hour as the light faded, there was a hatch of yellow mayfly. These are not dissimilar to our own mayfly. The fish go mad for those few minutes and the larger ones can be tempted. It is so exciting, but no time to get a tangle.

After a few days in angler's heaven it was time to move on. We had all caught lots of trout and Tal had the thrill of progressively catching a bigger trout each day than she'd ever caught before.

We arrived in Cordoba in time to go out for a late afternoon dove flight. I set off following Antonio my bird boy along a path through the bushes to a clearing. He set up a stool with a case of 500 cartridges and handed me the four-shot semi-auto Beretta 20 bore. You can imagine my reaction, as a traditional side-by-side shot. Yes I was sceptical, as I fed four No 8 shot Rio cartridges into the magazine. However as soon as doves appeared in the air, the gun seemed to leap into action, the trigger finger did not need to be told what to do, and the first doves came spinning down.

Nick is a marvellous host and spent time ensuring that everyone was getting some shooting. In the meantime Tal and Josephine had come with me and sat in folding chairs chatting. In due course Nick appeared and we stood 20 yards apart, getting our eyes in at these sporting little birds. It was such fun shooting together, watching and sharing the joy of each other's shots. Shouts, hollers or whistles of excitement may not have been the form on a formal day's game shooting at home, but here it did not seem out of place. The two girls sat behind like two nannies in the park, only interrupting their conversation to give us occasional words of encouragement, as like two little boys we played excitedly.

The hospitality of Manuel and Octavio and all who run the very successful enterprise was magnificent. On the second day it rained in the morning but it did not prevent the doves from flighting. These birds are 'mourning doves', about the size of blackbirds and they fly like our collared doves, but faster. Most parties shoot in or near the feeding fields of sorghum but Nick arranged it so that most of our shooting was in the hills. This terrain produced such a great variety of quality sport. One afternoon I had an extreme grouse-type shoot with birds flashing over the scrubby thorns, which are the predominant vegetation on these steep hills. It was like a three-hour game of squash, having to be ready every moment for the next dove as it flashed past. The little Beretta 20 bore semi-auto was, I have to reluctantly admit, very light and fast to handle. Can you imagine a grouse drive that goes on for three hours? There are enormous numbers of these doves and they are a plague to farmers.

After the first afternoon I was to find that the others had their bird boys loading their guns for them, which was apparently normal. So, with Antonio seated on my right, he was able to keep popping cartridges in and all the while continuing to click on his counter the birds which I had shot.

Dove shooting in Cordoba is perhaps the ultimate shooting-abroad experience. All in all it was a trip that combined the best of country sport, hospitality, food and sunshine, but as always in life what really made it were the special friends who bring all those shared joys together.

Life in the Old Dog Yet

As you know, where pigeons are concerned my preference is more for shooting grey ones than clay ones. My competitive spirit is more to improve my own shooting than compete with others. However it had been several years since entering for any of the major side-by-side competitions, so a day out for the Beesley and grandfather's hammer Purdey seemed a good idea. We arrived at the West Wycombe shooting ground for the European side-by-side championships – a grand title for a competition not heard of by any European east of Kent.

It was a hundred-bird layout over twelve varied stands representing all sporting quarry, driven or walked up. Within a minute of arriving, I was aware of a good atmosphere amongst a great variety of characters – groups from clubs, gangs from the East End – though none with sawn-off barrels. There were sporting gentlemen, competition internationals having a day out with a side-by-side for fun, and a number of oddball pigeon decoy men like myself. A nice man hidden behind a whiskery beard and moustache (as well as head to toe tattoos) came over for a chat. A keen pigeon shooter, he would certainly be very camouflaged in any hedgerow.

Mr Beesley came with me on the first round. We found a steady driven pair to start with, which boosted our confidence. Then we took the stands as they appeared. The simultaneous, angled going-away pair were not my favourites but Beesley saw them as departing pigeon and they dropped to shot. A rabbit followed by a fast, looping battue got the same treatment. However after such a good start some driven crossers sailed on and my card began to look ragged.

Passing the pool shoot it seemed there was nothing to lose by having a go. It was a 16-bird grouse complex. There was nobody in front of me so it had to be shot blind. This was fine and old Beesley may have been born in 1906 but he jumped into action for these exciting targets and killed the lot. I don't know who was the more surprised – me, Beesley or the nice chaps on the stand.

With encouragement we continued as a good partnership and completed the competition with a round of eighty-six; good for me (although Beesley said he could have done better).

After a break and a chat Mr Purdey came out. Compared with Beesley who weighs 7 pounds 13 ounces, Purdey is a flyweight at 6 pounds 5 ounces. He jumps into action and is so fast into the shoulder in spite of his age, having been born in 1887. The result was that we shot well at different stands from those in the earlier round and dropped birds at other stands straighted before. An interesting experience but Mr Purdey was not to be out-shot by his younger companion and also put in a round of eighty-six which stood well in the hammer gun class.

It was more like a day out than a competition: and so it was for Richard Faulds and Tanya, who arrived at lunch time with a borrowed Beretta side-by-side provided by his sponsors. He had just returned from winning the world FITASC in Cyprus with an amazingly high score. However to use a side-by-side (and one never in his hands before) was like shooting with one arm tied behind his back – or could have been for any normal shot. However to Richard it was a mere inconvenience and to watch him was a lesson indeed. His calm, rhythmical style rises from the tips of his toes up through his whole body and out with the shot from the tip of the muzzle. He is co-ordinated with total focus from the first sight of the target until it is smashed. He never appears hurried nor looks awkward at any stage. He was never fazed when on rare occasions he missed a target with this odd gun. He was just so laid back and wandered in with a score of 91 in spite of the handicaps – with his own gun I doubt he would have missed at all. I would have travelled there just for the joy of watching him.

Tanya then used this gun and in spite of the same handicaps as Richard, shot well enough to win the ladies' prize: a great example to her clients at Bisley shooting ground.

At the end of the day nobody else had shot the grouse sequence straight (not even my hero Richard Faulds) and so the pool kitty paid for my day out. More than that, Mr Purdey's score was only one away from winning the hammer gun class but with a proud second prize: yes you've guessed it – a year's subscription to the *Shooting Gazette*.

Forging a Link from His Past to the Future

Archie Coats in action

Of the many people we encounter in life a few will become key formative figures. For me Archie Coats, father of pigeon shooting, was one of those people. So it was a joy to welcome his grandson, appropriately named Archie after his grandfather, to stay for two days. It was an opportunity to introduce him to pigeon decoying and to the sport of angling for carp. Young Archie was then nearly fourteen, but had sadly never known his namesake who died before he was born. Young Archie arrived with Prue Coats his grandmother who, as a close friend, is a frequently welcome visitor.

Young Archie is a very intelligent lad, way beyond his years. Wine, history, cricket or politics are subjects of which he has encyclopaedic knowledge and surprisingly mature opinions and, like most youths, he has a mental and physical dexterity about all modern technology. My wife Gina produced a special lunch, the main meal of the day as we planned to go carp fishing in the evening. While granny had a nap after lunch, Archie came with me on a reconnaissance trip around prospective rape stubbles for decoying the next day. It is important to show youngsters the background of sport.

After tea and with a car full of rods and tackle tangled between Prue and Arch, we set off to the carp lake. A warm evening found them on the surface feeding well: like slow-motion trout they rose from the depths to suck in the dog-food pellets we tossed in as tasters. These carp have become very clever at teasing the bait from the hook without taking the latter. Young Arch was soon jumping up and down with frustration as time and time again the carp teased him into believing they had swallowed the hook. We stood and fished side by side. For a while he still had not quite got the knack of hooking them and he kept saying I was lucky. Then he decided I was fishing on the best side – so we swapped. Then he decided I must have the best rod – so we swapped. Eventually he got the hang of hooking them and realised that skill overcame the choice of rod or position! A lesson was learnt and Isaac Walton had another disciple of the art of angling.

Next morning saw a visit to Sam Grice at his Long Acres shooting ground (the most inspiring coach for young shots in the land). Young Arch shoots with a 20 bore and with central vision needs to close his left eye at the moment prior to taking the shot. Sam soon had him consistently smashing driven clays. The genes of his grandfather, the finest game shot I have ever seen, are obviously inherited; practice and experience will do the rest.

A quick pit stop at home to swap granny for pigeon kit and off we went to try decoying pigeon. The chosen field was watched for a while to decide on the best place for a hide. With a footpath along one side we had to shoot from the other, but it was not ideal for wind though it did have a good hedge in which to make a hide. The key to safety in a double hide is to have a pole between the Guns as a barrier to limit the swing of a gun, and for only one person to shoot at a time.

There was not as much traffic to the field as we had seen on the day before but soon a few birds were decoying well. It was not long before Archie shot his first ever decoyed pigeon as it crossed from left to right. We celebrated immediately with a photograph to record the achievement. Then there was a spell of unaccountable misses as birds at times hovered invitingly over the decoys. I stood behind him and watched a few shots which were not co-ordinated. I then asked him to shoot at a static dead bird decoy and the cloud of dust was four feet to the left. What had happened to the Coats' genes of the morning? 'Ah,' said young Arch, 'I've been shutting my wrong eye!' For a moment I thought he had lost his genetic intelligence as well. However, once this was recovered and his correct eye shut, the next shot dissolved the decoy in a cloud of dust and feathers. We were back in action and more good shots were added to our bag. We had both learned a lot and became good friends – for me it was a joy to share and create a sporting link from grandfather to the grandson he never knew.

When Reality Exceeds Expectation

A year or two ago my few special grouse shooting invitations had one by one all been cancelled. The reason being the disastrous decline of stock over the previous winter and spring due to wet weather and high worm burdens. This was the result of an exceptionally good season the year before when excessive grouse stocks caused a more severe crash than would be usual after the peak of a grouse cycle. So many moors would not shoot that season and some may not have a shootable surplus for several years, however good the management and keepering.

I was seeing and hearing about the situation first-hand while I was painting a landscape commission on Burnhope moor in upper Weardale. For four days I had good weather and could paint the beck that flowed off the moor over the layered rocks, creating an attractive waterfall. The heather-clad moorland stretched to the horizon in all directions, but I didn't hear or see any sign of a grouse. In sympathy I painted the head of a single old cock, peering like a periscope around the heather. With sad sarcasm the painting has become titled *Artistic Licence*.

However Stephen Catlin owns a second moor about 15 miles away just into Cumbria. Ousby moor is keepered by an enthusiastic young man named Philip Robinson who reported that he had some grouse, in fact good broods from above average spring pair counts. 'Nay lad,' said all the old keepers around him, 'nobody has grouse – all shooting's cancelled. You can't have grouse, stop imagining things.' This went on all summer but eventually, after the July counts, Phil still said he had grouse and his headkeeper Dougy Johnson agreed it was worth having a day.

Sometimes the itinerant artist is lucky being in the right place at the right time! As I arrived off the barren Burnhope moor with my painting that evening I was invited to shoot.

Apologies for what could be a disappointing day were expressed by our host at dinner the evening before but we were all thrilled just to have the chance of a day's driven grouse this season.

The day was bright with a light breeze. Clouds cast shadows across the fells and slid across the contours. Yes there were grouse and some really good coveys in each of the three morning drives, offering sporting shots as they came through the line of butts. No bird stimulates the adrenaline of the shooting man more than those wild, dark birds that hug the contours, appear from nowhere and in a moment are gone. Like the deft magician's trick of illusion – now you see them, now you don't.

The mood in the lunch hut was upbeat after such a good morning with sixty-one brace in the bag. We would have been delighted with that at the end of the day.

The first drive after lunch was an even greater surprise and I was in No. 4 butt. A few early birds produced a shot or two and then coveys and odd birds came steadily to me. Robert Morley was good company loading for me, and his dry sense of humour bubbled up all day. I was having a good drive and with fifteen spent cartridge cases on the butt in front of Robert, all set in the direction of the corresponding birds' fall, he quietly said he thought I was getting my eye in a bit. Little did we know, as we could not see the beaters over the short skyline, that it was only halfway through the drive. But a good drive was to become a great one and by the horn there were thirty-one cases representing birds to pick.

EVERYONE CAN DO SOMETHING TO HELP WILDLIFE

Our local paper the Cambridge Evening News dispatched a feature writer and photographer to interview me and look round my mini shoot at the time of the publication of my book *Will's Shoot Revisited*. I was interested to see what angle the young lady, Sarah O'Meara, would want to write about and was concerned as to how the shoot would be portrayed. I was pleasantly surprised at her encouraging attitude to this and her spontaneous grasp of the connection between the shoot management and the benefits to all wildlife. For me the abandoned gravel workings at Hauxton pits have been a wonderful challenge and opportunity, since acquiring the original 69 acres in 1970, to develop my passion for the link between wildlife management and that of fishing and shooting. My dual hats as keeper of the shoot and warden of the sanctuary worked symbiotically to the benefit of game, fish and all ecology. As a boy brought up in the country it all seemed so obvious but at that time there were definitely two sides and they rarely met in the middle. The word 'conservation', was not yet in use and gamekeepers were considered by the public to be friends to game but enemies of wildlife. However, on the contrary, keepers in so many ways have been the unsung heroes of the conservation movement. The better they and landowners managed habitat for game the more prolific the wildlife on those shoots.

Luckily most aware people now understand this and all the organisations working for country sports have embraced this fully. The Game and Wildlife Conservation Trust have evolved from purely game management to fully integrated habitat and species research. WAGBI became the British Association for Shooting and Conservation. Sadly not all the wildlife organisations have

The final drive was good and by then all were euphoric: guns, beaters, flankers and pickers-up alike. What a day it had been, but the man with the justifiably proudest smile was young Phil Robinson, the keeper himself. Unbelievably the total was 145 brace – a record for the moor. At last Phil's grouse were proved real and the keepers in the area stopped saying he was dreaming. With a high young to old count of 4:1, that represented an average covey of ten birds. For most grouse keepers that would be a dream in any season. The guns had shot well with a 2.2:1 average. The whole experience was the greater taking place in such a year of doom for grouse generally. There was not another moor in the land which produced a record day that season. A rare record indeed. If joy is felt when reality exceeds expectation, then that was it.

understood the benefits that the management of a shooting interest brings though the county wildlife trusts have come a long way in appreciating this. However the leading organisation for the protection of birds is still Dickensian in its obstinacy to acknowledge the fact that keepered areas, whether moorland or lowground, have more birds than certain areas of similar habitats on their reserves where predators are uncontrolled.

However, I digress and must focus again on my little patch of about 85 acres of south Cambridgeshire. The point is that the scale is immaterial and my project at Hauxton is small as a shoot; large if one thinks of it as a wildlife and sporting garden; vast if compared with a small suburban garden but tiny when compared with grand estates of tens of thousands of acres.

It's true that most of us, whether knowingly or not, have the opportunity to do something irrespective of scale. The principles are the same, whether managing a window box or grand acres to create a variety of habitats and work with nature not against it. The editor of the local paper embraced this point and asked me to draw up a 10-point list of how readers could benefit wildlife. There was good feedback from this and it stimulated thought. Interestingly there were no irate letters following my piece of advice on predators*. Similarly on visits to Hauxton by groups of the public it is encouraging that when I explain freely and openly how the management for game and wildlife are of mutual benefit, I never have a problem. The difficulties come from those who do not understand or who are not prepared to listen to the message.

*Acknowledge that all species of wildlife have predators. It is unkind to welcome all the birds to your garden and then allow your cat out to kill them. Rats, squirrels and magpies will all eat eggs and young birds in the nest. We cannot be blinkered to our responsibilities as wildlife managers, to protect the species we wish to encourage.

The Nightmare Scenario

The first single partridge came from afar, was successfully flanked into the drive and as it approached me on the end of the line it rose high in the blue sky before banking to make an exciting shot over my right shoulder. I had waited for a quarter of an hour with excitement and anticipation for such a moment. I was all ready for the action. Having assessed height, speed, angle and line as I mounted my gun, I pulled the trigger and . . . click-click. Yes, I'd done everything but actually load my musket. With the other seven Guns spectating that first lone bird of the drive, a minor nightmare for me was, of course, the cause of great laughter for them.

The shooter's ultimate nightmare is of running out of cartridges on a special drive or big day's pigeon shoot – or so I thought until a dream I had recently . . .

A good line of pigeon was coming to a certain 'sitty' tree, near which I had made my hide to intercept the birds approaching or decoy them within range. Nothing odd about that to the conscious mind by day, or subconscious mind by night. However the tree in the dream was not out in the countryside but in the centre of a courtyard, the hallowed ground of a University College or cathedral, surrounded by tall classical buildings, one of which was certainly ecclesiastical with stained-glass windows. My sitty tree was a fine spreading cedar and my hide was made in a rare species of shrub, all set on a pristine lawn. My decoys showed up well on the short grass with smart light and dark stripes of the morning cut by Mr Atco's sharpened blades.

Pigeons started to come from over the buildings, making very sporting shots high in the sky, but frustratingly none of the bodies hit the ground. They either lodged in the canopy of the cedar or landed on rooftops and rolled into hidden gutters behind parapets. Then one nearly smashed through the stained-glass window only to lodge behind a fancy architectural feature thirty feet above the ground. Yet another crashed into a gargoyle, that ghoulishly dripped blood onto those below.

At times there were many people, some in gowns others, perhaps sightseers, keeping carefully to the York stone pavement surrounding the sharp-edged lawn with little square signs every few yards telling people to 'keep off the grass'. Such instructions were obviously not intended for the lone pigeon shooter and his dog hidden in the shrub, that had been suitably but sacrilegiously chopped about as if it was a common elder bush in a hedgerow.

Those pigeon, which swooped down to approach the decoys set up so seductively on the lawn, were frustratingly unshootable, as at no point of their flight were they without a background of windows in the surrounding architecture. So the nightmare continued. About noon two men in uniforms rolled out a red carpet from the cloisters on one side of the courtyard to the entrance of the chapel on the other side. As this pigeon-scaring carpet rolled passed my hide I came out to move the decoys to one side, rather as one does if a tractor comes to roll a field of newly drilled barley. I asked what was happening: 'Oh,' said one, 'the bishop is coming this afternoon to consecrate a new memorial in the chapel and the courtyard will be filled with hundreds of people for the occasion.' So much for the solitude of the lone decoyer.

The next pigeon flew over and, when shot, did not land on the roof but crashed to ground, landing thump on the red carpet. The blood did not show up but the cascade of grey feathers did. I suddenly awoke – no please do not send any dream analysis – pigeon shooting is often not easy in the real world without knowing more about the twisted sleeping mind of a certain pigeon shooter.

Not a Sport for the Faint-hearted

Max and Tim are chums who I know through our mutual interest in fishery management. They run an amazing shoot on a forgotten part of coastal east Essex. The Vikings may have landed there but few others since. It is a world of overgrown old woods where oak, ash, sweet chestnut and sycamore tangle in their fight for light. Below is a bramble, bracken and rhododendron thicket, with primeval bog in the hollows. The woodland is interspersed with undrained boggy meadows and on the higher land there is conventional arable farming. It is the most wonderful habitat for a great variety of game, wildfowl and wildlife.

To be polite it could be called a very rough walking shoot. Guns are invited for their fitness, dogs, stamina, determination and ability to shoot through the thicket or vegetation. Somewhere on the 1,500 acres is a quarry species at which you may just get the opportunity of a safe shot it you are sharp-eyed through 360 degrees from dawn 'til dusk.

Twelve of us, privileged to come through the tough selection process, were invited on a day in early December. A briefing from Max and then off to a speculative duck drive should any migrant wildfowl be on the old decoy pond. Suddenly the air was a whisper as gadwall climbed over the tall oaks and above them teal virtually out of shot. Hardly surprising that we were more successful with the gadwall and thirteen were picked as against just two teal. Simultaneously half the Guns had gone to drive the little reservoir and returned with a tufted duck and two greylags. A successful start indeed.

Then the first big manoeuvre as we were in groups starting to hunt and blank in vast acres of arable to an area of thick hedgerows and marsh. Half a mile away odd shots were indicating the other team's approach. Eventually the bramble clump at the heart of the whole exercise was surrounded and the wild pheasants which, when flushed by Max's Jack Russell, rocketed out in all directions producing very sporting driven shots.

Then coffee and delicious icing-topped pastries boosted the blood sugar levels before we split into groups to walk a large woodland on either side of a brook which ended in the ponds and lakes of the old decoy. I was instructed to follow the edge of the water to get a chance of coot or waterhen. Conon and I hunted the right bank without sight or sound of anything but a squirrel which tantalisingly disappeared into the hole of a tree without the chance of a shot. Suddenly my right boot sank into stinking mud, my left boot with all my weight slid below the surface, and without any resistance, I was disappearing into bottomless black slime. I had to brace myself on my old Beesley – flat on the surface – to prevent a tragedy culminating in my glutinous end. It gave me a chance to grab a sallow branch overhead and pull myself out. It was a lucky escape with just a bootfull of black sludge, the tidemark of which was nearly up to my waist. It was all worthwhile as Conon then flushed a hen pheasant which was added to the bag.

Mulligatawny soup and pork pie made a quick lunch, then we were off again on another big manoeuvre. I was put as the one Gun in the epicentre of the exercise. This was on the point of two woods that met at the corner. The wind was right for pigeons to flight across my corner. I hid up in a thicket and during the hour-long manoeuvre fifteen pigeons and a carrion crow made my contribution to the bag.

It was dark by the time the last team arrived from the final wood back at the decoyman's old cottage. Game bags were disembowelled and triumphant stories were told of each hard-earned trophy. What a bag it was – with eighteen species and a record total of 159 head. This was made up of thirty-three pheasants, three red-legged partridges, five woodcock, six carrion crows, two teal, thirteen gadwall, one tufted duck, two greylag geese, six rabbits, one hare, one squirrel, seventy-nine woodpigeons, one collared dove, one herring gull, one jackdaw, two rooks, one jay and a magpie. A great day indeed, where any step could be your last or could produce the shot of a lifetime.

Undeserved Luck

You won't believe it but – yes I left my gun at home again. I thought the lesson would have been learned a year or two ago when I turned up at the first shoot of the season and opened the back of the car, in which there was no gun but my dog and a strimmer collected from the mower man on the way. 'Not very complimentary to your host's partridges', laughed my mates.

On this occasion, a few miles from the shoot I looked over my shoulder – no gun on the back seat – panic. To return home would take me at least forty-five minutes and I would be very late. I tried phoning my host but he'd left home with no mobile so I could not warn him of my predicament.

Suddenly I had an idea and phoned Brian who helps with the keepering and is my right-hand man at Hauxton. Yes he was still at home, yes I could borrow a gun. I rally-drove the ten minutes back to his house, which saved a crucial extra twenty minutes round trip. Then I zoomed back and rolled into the yard only five minutes late with apologies to my host who, luckily, was more amused than annoyed. The fellow Guns on this smart shoot enquired as to whether my keeper's gun was a semi-auto in cammo colours? Luckily when I peeped in the slip it was Brian's old 30" Cogswell & Harrison side-by-side.

I was on the end of the line for the first drive. The main action was over the middle but then a small group of redlegs came my way. I made a slow, deliberate shot and the first bird flew into the pattern. Having turned, a second was taken as it went out behind. It felt no pain. This gun was a joy to use and fitted me perfectly and at the end of the drive six birds were picked for as many shots.

On the second drive at number two I had one of the best pegs, being on the downwind end of the line. It was a long drive and partridges came from way back rising all the way as they approached the guns. The old Cogswell had a life of its own and jumped into action with Exocet-accuracy. We went sixteen straight before missing a high bird behind my neighbour. I did not seem to do anything, the gun just knew where to go. The rest of the day I had a magic draw and was in the shooting. Those fellow Guns who earlier laughed at my stupidity were becoming indignant at the injustice of the situation. To have laughed all day at my missing with a borrowed gun would have been fun. However to find the gun shot better than my own and that I enjoyed a disproportionate amount of the sport each drive was not so funny. My neighbour's comment was: 'Was I going to offer my keeper a good price for it?'

The penultimate drive capped it all when out on the end of the line I was on the other side of an intersecting hedge. Normally the birds come over a tall hedge in front of the rest of the Guns who stand well back. However that week the hedging contractor had misunderstood instructions and had flailed it down. The result was the birds flew forward and banked downwind, out of shot of the line of Guns who acted like flankers. The partridges then rose and came over the tall hedge on my right, which was the one that should have been cut low. So a steady stream of partridge came in ones and twos and then rose to make great shooting for me. With embarrassment I appeared from behind my hedge at the end of the drive with two handfuls of birds and was flanked by two beaters similarly laden.

At the end of such a good day Brian's old Cogswell contributed an embarrassing ninety-nine birds of the total bag of 245 for the nine Guns. So a generous thanks to the keeper and I may want to borrow Brian's lucky gun again. Who knows, he may do well hiring it out to readers of this book.

Even the Bad Times are Good

It had been a long week and I needed a day of pigeon shooting, my favourite way of communing with nature and putting the world to right. So I set off to a favourite area, an estate where I have been fortunate to shoot game for years and always so enjoy my days.

There were fewer pigeon than normal this February but one good day on a chopped maize strip and another on a field of spring drilling inspired me to go and look round this particular Saturday. The drilling had long finished and the maize strips were bare. However I can usually squeeze a bag of pigeon from somewhere unusual or a flight line. Bill, the keeper, said that he had not seen much about and, after an hour of checking out likely places, I had to agree. However, in the distance a few shots could be heard.

I drove round searching the likely sitty woods or belts of trees for indication of things to come, when from midday onwards birds were thinking of feeding. Nothing caught my eye. A handful clattered out of a beech tree along the track but they drifted aimlessly on the wind over the horizon. It was still only mid-morning and parking on a hill to watch over a long vista, I drew a cup of coffee from the flask. I nibbled on a leathery Kit-Kat bought at a filling station on the way for which I had failed to notice the sell-by date, which like the game on the estate had been six weeks ago. I'm always amused by products that display in bold print; 'best before end' – that too relates to the shooting season – even life itself! Too much philosophy and not enough pigeon seemed to be increasingly obvious.

When I caught up with Bill, who was out ferreting, he told me that the maize strips on the neighbouring estate had only been chopped that week. Obviously this had drawn the pigeons and the boys were getting their turn of some good sport.

It is rare for me to go pigeon shooting purely on spec without a prior recce but the day was a bonus and so my expectations had not been high. It was getting on for 2 p.m. before I saw a hint of any pigeon traffic, let alone a place worth setting up. Then on the corner of a maize strip that had been chopped weeks ago, I saw a handful of birds feeding and a few more in a clump of trees in a pit at one end. Then another joined them. Other birds were in trees along the woodside at the other end of the strip.

Memories were kindled as I had had an amazing day last year on this maize, shooting in a south-westerly wind, ideal for the trees in the pit. However this wind was a strong easterly, which would not be good for that end but it could work from the edge of the wood, especially as one or two more birds had flown over two particular beech trees on the same line.

I decided to give it a go as there was nothing to excite me elsewhere and there was only an hour or two left of the pigeon-feeding day. A hide was easily established in a position to give the optimum arc of fire. Decoys and the rotary were set up on the stubble. This was about 60 yards from the nearest edge of the maize strip but should birds come to the maize I felt I could draw them to my position on the sporadic flight line over the wood.

The first customer came wide to my right. It showed absolutely no recognition of the decoys but was unlucky enough to pass an opening in the trees and crashed down further back in the wood making an easy retrieve for Conon.

A few minutes later a pigeon produced a mirror image shot on the left, another suddenly appeared across my front along the wood making for a spontaneous shot. I was up the left-hand side of it but it collapsed with a broken wing.

Then a lull before an overhead incomer was followed by a downwinder from behind which must have been sitting in the trees. From my left, one actually decoyed, swooping round low making a straightforward shot. Later I missed an easy crosser then killed a high one through the trees which made up for it.

Every shot was so different and after two hours of not-brisk sport, but with a shot every five minutes or so, I had experienced a shoot of extreme variety. There had been a challenge and the great satisfaction was of making something from nothing. It was a modest bag of twenty-three but each had its own story and had produced a most memorable and enjoyable day. Driving happily home I was reminded of the sportsman's true saying: 'It's not what you go out to get but what you get out of going.'

A Dawn Celebration of Fifty Years

The 5th May was the day, fifty years ago, that when I was a child aged eleven, the family moved into the house that is still my home in Cambridgeshire. I awoke early that first morning and the sound of the 'dawn chorus' made me think I'd come to heaven. I did not know what birds they were except for the cuckoo, which was obvious, but the cacophony of sound was more musical than any orchestra. All strange for a young boy who by day, was always in trouble and by night slept so soundly, rekindling the energy for wickedness the next day.

To commemorate the fifty-year anniversary my alarm clock was set for 4 a.m. With a cup of tea, binoculars and a notebook I sat on a bench in the garden in silent darkness. However just as I realised I had mistimed my enthusiasm for dawn, the first sound reached my ears from far away. It was none other than the skylark somewhere out over the fields. Could this really be true, at ten past four in pre-dawn darkness? But there it was, all on its own making true the saying that 'up with the lark' is truly early.

As a glimmer of light was discernible the first rooks stirred. There are about thirty nests in the trees around the drive and the young were fledged sufficiently for some to be seen perched on or around their nest by day. The raucous sound of the parents became an agitated crescendo before they flew to start their early morning search for food for the young. The territorial call from a cock pheasant, the first coo, coo, coo, coo-coo from my favourite, the woodpigeon, and then the plaintive song of the robin. All this whilst it was still too dark to make any notes or see through my bino's. The pair of tawny owls were also very vocal and active as they prepared to nest in the roadside trees beyond the paddock where the first bleats of ewes could be heard as they reassured their lambs.

Then the magic moment as the main musicians responded to dawn's conductor in the sky. The blackbirds and thrushes, as if from every shrub, bush and tree in the parish, in unison created the sound that is unique as the 'dawn chorus'. There were such uplifting, optimistic and enthusiastic combinations of songs that touched my heart, as much on that morning as they did all those years ago as a child. I could now just read my watch: 4.43 a.m. A wren trilled from the depths of a clump of ivy. A red-legged partridge called from away on the hill 'chuck-chuck-chuckerr'. At that moment I passed the dustbin shed, the home of our pair of swallows – they swirled out together in aerial synchronised flight, then amazingly alighted on the top of my car and mated. In a moment consummation was complete and they were away up in the sky, where they took a light honeymoon breakfast of insects.

So many birds do not start to sing until after sunrise. This was about 5.20 a.m., when the tits could be heard everywhere and chaffinches, collared doves and hedge sparrows were all on song. Then the gentle purring of a turtle dove, the welcome harbinger of summer. A whitethroat in the hedge at the end of the old orchard and a blackcap and a chiffchaff represented the warblers. There were a number of little twittery sounds I could not identify, but a true ornithologist, with sharp, un-shot-out hearing would have listed them all. Another joy that day was to welcome back the spotted flycatcher.

Later that evening when my brother Guy and his wife Julia joined Gina and me for a drink, we exchanged early memories. We were all relaxed and almost emotional but just to burst the bubble, a magpie flew across the lawn and chuckled at us from the top of the lilac tree. I thought the Larsen trap had done its job but nature has a way of reasserting the balance, just as man falsely believes he's in control. There is always a lesson in life even after fifty years.

You Can Keep Your Cruises

Late June is when Gina and I spend a fortnight on a summer holiday, painting in the area of north Norfolk around our cottage. There is a heat haze across the marsh and the blue sea makes a good horizontal background to the landscape. A relaxing time but it just so happens that there is a gun, together with nets, decoys and cartridges hidden in the back of the car. I can usually squeeze a couple of sporting days pigeon shooting out of the landscape as well as a few paintings. This summer was no exception and produced two outstanding days.

There was a set-aside with barley growing among the grasses and thistles on a field nearby. Not only were pigeon feeding on it but others were passing over on a flight line out to fields beyond. Bernard Bishop, warden of Cley marsh, is also the keeper here and as a very old friend we've had a number of enjoyable days decoying together though never have we quite hit the right field at the right time. However, on this occasion things were to be different. He could join me at 1.30 p.m. but had to go to a wildfowlers' meeting in the evening. I set up a double hide and got things going, so when Bernie arrived he could get shooting.

In the hour before he came I had already shot fifty and it was even better sport than anticipated. We were both soon taking birds on our respective sides. The exciting thing was that we had a lot of birds coming downwind from woods out to the left. They passed over fast at various heights and on occasion we saw a pair coming and took one each simultaneously with an imperceptible pause between the b-bang of our two shots. The two dead birds would hit the ground together. Other pigeons came silently from behind, sliding out over the decoys making awkward shots, but we were both on good form. This was by far the best day we had shared together in over thirty years. It was very special for us both and by the time Bernard had to leave for his meeting we had another 163 birds on the clicker. I carried on for the evening and, though the action slowed down, another fifty were added to the bag before the long job of picking-up.

I thought things could not get better. All the barley in the area was thin due to the lack of rain in the light sandy soil. However, there was a field of barley further east along the coast. It was a narrow field beside a lane that led out to the marsh and sea where, in the valley bottom, the soil was more fertile and with a heavy crop some had gone down. For several days I had watched a good number of pigeon, buzzing like flies over these laid patches.

It was not an easy field to shoot. With a public right of way along the track I had to make a hide out in the field and shoot safely in the opposite direction and away from the village, which was nearby. It would be a noisy day so I called in at the village school to inform them of shooting next day. Luckily, as a country school, this was not met with the problems likely to be encountered elsewhere. I was not prepared to shoot in a field of standing corn unless there could be help picking-up as old Conon would go till he dropped and young Scott is only allowed a few retrieves in his training. Thankfully Robin, the headkeeper, arranged to come that evening with Paddy who has a good team of retrievers.

With a hide in the crop, thatched with barley, the first birds were already circling the field. Having to shoot away from the footpath and the village meant that the wind was all wrong, and blowing straight into the hide. Therefore birds came unseen from behind me and would just appear over my left or right shoulder, sliding out away from me, making awkward long going-away quartering targets.

However, it was busy from the moment of the first shot at midday until 7 p.m. when it was time to pick up. For the seven hours of hectic shooting, over a pigeon a minute foolishly flew into the shot.

Robin and Paddy arrived and with nine dogs between us it was an exhausting job for all. We took several sack loads off the field and then rested the dogs by a cool stream where I had hidden three cans of beer. Refreshed we went back and in the cool of the evening ended with a very successful pick-up two and a half hours after the last shot had been fired.

With the wonderful weather, both the painting and the pigeon shooting were a joy on this memorable holiday. Brochures of expensive cruises will continue to go in the bin.

WATER WINGS

Scott's training had been going well. His response to whistle and hand signals had become more positive by the day as our teamwork strengthened. He was then 18 months old and was allowed a few pigeon retrieves at the end of the day having sat happily for hours behind me in a pigeion hide. A contented and intelligent new companion.

June was a good time to start the boy on water work, but never did I expect the challenge that evolved. Playing in the shallows of the lake and retrieving dummies was all fine, but the thought of actually swimming was just too much for the poor chap. At first it seemed obvious that to gee him up, old Conon would do a couple of swim retrieves. Competition is a great come-on for the otherwise faint-hearted; but no, Scott just ran out until on tiptoes and happily let Conon do the retrieve. It made no difference if I sat him to wait or if I egged him on to just play and run in on the thrown dummy; he just did not fancy swimming.

Sometime in his life, Scott must have had a bad experience of water. It could have been in a dyke in March when he went into the water rather by mistake and it was cold and the bank was steep. Neither seemed to trouble him at the time but maybe it has lingered in his mind. I did notice that he was not swimming at all well with front legs splashing high out of the water and hindquarters low in the water, as if not working at all or maybe trying to touch the bottom. Whatever the situation, any dog of mine must retrieve and be confident in water on my little shoot at Hauxton with its several lakes and ponds and where even the woods are full of ribbons of water. So the summer challenge was on.

I felt the first thing to do was to keep him enjoying the play in the shallows: splashing about, retrieving or wallowing on hot days or watching Conon swimming. While water was fun confidence could overcome the mental block. The lakes got even warmer and even I was taking a swim every day but Scott could not be persuaded to follow me. I then decided to try him on the lead to give him confidence. While standing at a lead's length further from the shore when Scott was up to his shoulders, the dummy was tossed just beyond me. He was keen but still reluctant.

However as I gave enormous encouragement and at the same time gave a tug on the lead, he launched himself and made big clumsy strokes past me to the dummy. I walked out holding the lead high above the water so as not to tangle his legs and on return to the bank we were both happily excited. Another fun retrieve from the shallows and that was enough for the day.

Every day we went to repeat the exercise and on each occasion the pull on the lead was reduced, then only a tweak was needed. Also the distance progressed for the swim each day as the dummy was thrown a yard further.

At last the day dawned a month later when he launched himself while still on the lead but without any tweak at all.

Then, next day, no lead was necessary and on the following day I did not need to be in the water at all. We'd cracked it and laid the ghost of the deep. By September he was actually beginning to gain confidence which helped him swim properly without front feet splashing or hindquarters sinking. There was still a long way to go together but we were well on the journey – lucky, as the water by then was too cold for me.

Pigeons and the Public

A large triangular field of about 25 acres had been drilled with peas, and the seeds had gone in so well that, apart from a little on the headlands, none were left on top.

However, a phone call from Jamie the keeper informed me that surprisingly a number of pigeons were on the field one afternoon. I went next day to observe and indeed by 3 p.m. there were more than enough to get me excited.

Overnight I made plans as it was not straightforward. The three sides of the field were surrounded by footpaths. It was Easter Saturday and there could be people about.

It is never easy to set up in the centre of a field and fool pigeons to come near a new feature in the landscape. However, with a net hide surrounded by branches of white thorn flushed with early leaf, the overall appearance was softened. It was 11 a.m. when I had set out my fifteen dead decoys, together with two crows. A similar number of artificial decoys built the flock to what I hoped would be a convincing picture. Although the previous day I had noted that the pigeons on the field were focused around the edges where the few peas might be gleaned from the surface, I was relying on the headlands being disturbed by walkers like mobile flankers. In this way, I hoped to turn a negative into a positive but then I have always been an optimist – an essential characteristic of a pigeon shooter.

So the scene was set and indeed it was a pleasant morning. I had all the time in the world to watch the traffic on the motorway beyond the footpath on the southern side, the odd cloud in the sky and a man who took over an hour to walk his dog around the field. By midday I realised I had definitely either started too early, or worse, that the pigeons were going elsewhere to feed. By 1 p.m. little had changed with only two shots at birds passing wide.

As occupational therapy, I had a spare clicker counting people who appeared on any of the three paths around the field. Yes, it was that boring but anything helped pass the time. There were twenty-two on the people clicker with only two on the one for pigeons. Then the pigeon traffic picked up in the lunch hour, and so by 2 p.m. the score was thirty-two people to twenty-nine pigeons. Could the pigeons win I wondered as a party of nine parents and children appeared on bikes? An elderly couple with a dog were going around the field in the opposite direction to a young lady with two doddery old labradors. However, the pigeons did the desired thing and floated out on a line to me in the centre of the field. Many decoyed surprisingly well but I had to pick my shots to angle them away from people or the motorway.

My decoys were set so I could shoot towards one corner of the field which was maybe 600 yards away, well out of shot, though the middle of each side of the triangle was half that distance. Whilst perfectly safe, it was important not to frighten or upset anyone. Luckily there was not a problem and few people even looked up when a shot was fired.

A gang of student joggers was followed by two horses with riders. However, although the pigeon traffic was easing down their count was ahead by 3.30 p.m. at 52:49 in favour of the pigeons. Later a line of birds came over high from behind. Some were just in range and made very satisfying shots, others passed wide but a few decided to snack on their way home and took a wide circle into the decoys.

My pattern was now convincing with maybe sixty fresh birds set up accompanying the original ones. I reached ninety on my clicker and whilst this was double my optimistic hope for the day I hung on for another hour and just made the magic one hundred. The total public count was sixty-six and they had done a great job keeping the pigeons from landing on the edges. I picked up ninety-four (pigeons that is) together with a couple of crows.

In any pigeon shooting book this experience would come in the chapter on advanced decoying and, like some television demonstrations, it should be added that this should not be tried at home.

Nocturnal Sounds of the Marsh

It was dusk on a fine but overcast evening in May, and I was accompanying Bernard Bishop as we tiptoed along the path out to the hide in the centre of the reserve to wait for a rogue fox that was threatening the ground-nesting birds all around us.

Avocets, godwits, gulls, terns and waders were nesting on the low islands which seemed to float in the shallow lagoons of carefully managed scrapes. Duck, geese, snipe and redshank in the margins, harriers and bitterns in the reed beds, lapwings, pipits and larks on the open grazed marsh. This was not the time or place for a fox to be allowed free meals.

Bernard is a true protector of his birds, like his father and grandfather who were wardens of the Cley marsh. Not only does he ensure the habitat and water levels are managed throughout the year, but he does all that is possible to legally protect them from predation.

The .22-250 rifle was set up on the ledge in the hide. Bernard had a spotting night vision scope with which the vigil was kept, watching over the area where, for two nights previously, the dead rabbit bait had been taken. The rifle itself has a high definition night sight, which picks up amazing detail, so the villain never knows of the presence or threat of the marksman and an efficient job can be done.

The sky was reflected in the glassy water before us and as darkness fell the banks, islands, and reed beds progressively merged into one abstract shape. Most bird species of garden, farm or forest fall silent at night but those of the wetland and marsh are late to bed. The sounds around us that night were so rich and varied. Geese with raucous comments in their neighbourly disputes, the piping of redshank, low toned 'waack – waack' of mallard in the reeds, and a snipe drummed overhead louder than a distant car on a coast road. The gentle breeze from the west softened the booming of the bittern which was regularly announcing its territory in the thickest reed beds. Like a foghorn it emanated eerily from a source that could be heard but not seen. Lapwings continued a constant aerial display and their 'peewit' was high pitched enough for even us 'shot deaf' countrymen to hear from afar. Bats flickered in and out of sight and a water vole swam past without sound or ripple.

Suddenly Bernard nudged me, passed the spotting scope and with excited agitation he took up the rifle. I could see nothing but the night vision monotone, green luminescence which appeared to blanket the scene. Water, reeds and grass but no fox could I see. Bernard's body language went from excitement to frustration then calm as the fox he had seen for a moment had melted back into the reeds.

Later the avocets began to murmur in short agitated piping calls, not urgent alarm but warning of a possible distant threat. Then a minute or two later my peripheral vision was drawn to a dark shape silhouetted, soft toned as it moved silently along the bank only 30 yards to my right. I nudged Bernard whose gaze faced the bait area through his spotting scope but by the time he had changed viewing angle the fox had disappeared behind thick reeds. He had trotted past purposely in the direction of the bait 60 yards ahead on the other side of the fringe of the reeds, behind which he had faded in the gloaming as if the whole experience had been figment of imagination. Believe me he had been real and the avocets had known it as he had slipped past them in darkness. However, he never showed. After another hour we admitted defeat. There would be another night, and Bernard assured me the rogue would not be there by the end of the week.

As we retraced our steps the air was heavy with the dank scent of water and reed, so evocative of fen and wetland marsh. Darkness was now all but complete; no moon, just a few soft stars between the clouds. Even the lapwings were silent. The whole evening experience had been a special one of magical sights and sounds. Particularly the sounds which had been so much more meaningful than those of the Eurovision Song contest which broke the spell as I passed by an open cottage window on my walk back home.

Black Magic

'Can you be there by 7.30 a.m.?', asked Tim, having suggested a day culling some corvids that were plaguing the local pig farmer. Leaving home just after 6 a.m. it was an early journey to the wilds of Essex. Tim and pals run Framlingham Fisheries, an outfit that trades coarse fish and acts as a consultant on fishery management. George, a bright young man, had recently joined the team and he was also a keen shot, but this was his first experience of decoying crows.

Tim had obviously done his homework, and reconnaissance indicated two positions for pre-built bale hides. I was dropped off first and was impressed by the straw bale construction which was strategically placed. It was a palace comprising sixteen bales, with four high on edge around three sides and two at the front. A wooden bar acted as a lintel over the front of the two side walls and this supported the final two bales as a roof. The addition of a screen net across the front at a height one could look through but shoot over meant the shooter was hidden from all angles.

A group of fifteen dead rooks and crows were set up in front of my hide on the wide perimeter track around the pig units which were separated by low electric fences. Tim prefers to use an electric flapper rather than a rotary machine. He feels that both of a pair of crows will confidently come right in to produce the chance of a left and right.

Tim and George left me ensconced and almost before my gun was out of its slip a crow was approaching. I scrambled a cartridge into the breech and the first bird collapsed amongst the decoys.

Action was brisk as from over the wood ahead of me a steady line of corvids approached. They saw the decoys and responded like magic. This was certainly the main line and the big black birds came like planes into Heathrow scheduled every two minutes. Interestingly I had expected rooks to be the main species but when there was a lull and I went out to tidy up it became evident that, amazingly, virtually all the large corvids were carrion crows with as many jackdaws but hardly any rooks.

There were sporadic shots from George and Tim but nothing compared to the action in my hide. After two hours there were eighty on my clicker, and when Tim called on the walkie-talkie I suggested either I swap with one of them or they could join me. However, he said his position was beginning to get an increasing number of visitors and so he moved George into his hide. Tim went to look over the road where there were more fields of pigs with many corvids, and he found a good spot to decoy them. He was soon popping away purposefully.

So all was evening itself out and, as my line eased off, George's position became busy as the black varmints were sent back to him from Tim's new position. I have

never seen so many carrion crows and they decoyed well. The secret was to let the first of the pair come well in and then as it gave a confident raucous 'arrrk arrrk' pull the trigger. It would fall and then hopefully the second bird too as it back-pedalled in the air.

The jackdaws were incredibly acrobatic and though the first bird was a fairly straightforward shot, the second seemed to loop, dive and jink simultaneously, often making very testing shots indeed.

The day continued steadily for all three of us and we had all shot over a hundred each from our respective positions. A bag of 115 carrion crows, 185 jackdaws and forty rooks contributed to a total of 428 (including a number of pigeons and ferrals).

Young George had put up a very tidy performance, in fact as a team we had been very effective and the farmer was delighted that there would be considerably fewer thieves stealing the food intended for his pigs.

A Bit of Family Time

My generation grew up in the years of myxomatosis, the scourge of the rabbit population. Maybe it is because rabbits were rare in my boyhood days that I so enjoy sport with them now. The humble bunny has become the focus of a day or two each year on our annual father and son trip to Scotland. We have only missed one year since my son Henry was twelve and this was our nineteenth visit.

We stood ten yards apart as our host, Steve, slipped one of his jills into the burrow on a mound of closely cropped grass, nibbled short by generations of Aberdeenshire rabbits. Henry covered the escape route to the left down the hill to the derelict stone dyke whilst I covered the run to the next burrow on the right.

We waited like coiled springs with our guns ready to jump into spontaneous action. Concentration was intense as anticipation fuelled our adrenaline. Two ears, then a head showed from one hole – a scurry and the rabbit scuttled two yards before darting down the adjacent hole. All went quiet for a minute with no sign of life. Then suddenly from a hidden bolt-hole a frisky rabbit rocketed out and bounced down the hill. Henry's gun jumped into action but his first shot went left as the rabbit had side-stepped a tussock just as the lead was halfway down the barrel. However, the second trigger made a very satisfying long shot just before the rabbit reached safety.

Lackie, Steve's short-legged old black labrador, retrieved it and returned up the hill with the rabbit hanging in his jaws. With a quick zip of Steve's razor-sharp knife, the belly was opened; and following a flick of the wrist the gut was out on the grass, a meal for a buzzard that evening.

Occasionally a ferret made a kill and lay up in a burrow, leaving us to watch and wait. Whether enjoying the wild flowers around one's feet or the views of ripening barley in the glen and woods on the hills, which are topped by heather moorland, it was just a beautiful place to be.

As we worked our way along the hillside, most burrows had one or two rabbits at home and some had as many as seven or eight. This was a good year and we enjoyed the sport of ferreting at its best.

Steve kindly invites us to shoot on this farm where he has the rabbit shooting and he is brilliant at handling his team of ferrets. They are all very user-friendly so sometimes we split up and take a ferret each to cover more small burrows. If one of the jills gets sticky or cannot bolt the rabbit, Steve pops the big hob ferret down the hole – no rabbit takes him on.

At one stage of the day we work the ferrets along the derelict stone dyke at the bottom of the hill. This is exciting snap-shooting as many of the rabbits teasingly hole-hop rather than bolt. One has to be careful to ensure safety at all times and be extra careful of angles we shoot to avoid ricochets. There are few more satisfying shoots than a crossing rabbit, killed so it just somersaults head over heels. It is not a sport for the premeditated shooter as most of the shots taken are spontaneous. Quick reactions and good gun mounting are the secret.

At midday, in the warmth of the late summer sun, we loll on a grassy bank having our piece and a dram. Steve always has a brand of Speyside whisky that is as fiery as any that warms the spot and waters the eye.

The pleasure for Henry and me is that we share a sport where we can enjoy each other's company as we watch each rabbit bolt. It is a day of good teamwork and camaraderie of which great memories are made. It was a marvellous and successful day and as the bag was laid out we accounted for 108 rabbits and a pigeon. Nothing is wasted as Steve skins and butchers the rabbits and sells them along with venison meat products at the weekly farmers' market.

So the end of another special day's sport and a memory of a time together that nobody can take away.

Shooting with a Friend

Shoot hosts or syndicate captains each bring their own personality to the event. There are those who are formal, others laid back, some are control freaks, others leave the whole event for the keeper to organise. Each displays his own character and style of hospitality.

But then there is Barry. The only thing he has in common with all hosts is that he is very generous and, as a close shooting mate, invites me more often than I deserve to his fine shoot in Norfolk. However, after his greeting and brotherly hug, which is genuine, his twisted sense of humour provokes a Jekyll and Hyde trait to govern the rest of my day.

His greatest joy is for everything to go wrong for me. Whilst most hosts hope their guests have good shooting, Barry loves me to get as little as possible. Whilst guns on most shoots are moved up or down pegs to improve sport for guests, he likes nothing better than to ease me to Outer Mongolia.

My fun and challenge is to shoot my share of the bag against my host's schemes. Luckily my guardian angel is usually with me and birds fly out to me where they've never flown before. When I'm in the middle of the line he cannot interfere too much though he is known to move guns closer to me to squeeze me out. Either way, Barry will jump up and down with joy if his plans work or with frustration if they have not.

Now, do not get the idea that I am complaining, as I still get lots of shooting whatever, usually far more than he would like to make his day. I enjoy the challenges and he enjoys the mirth.

As he is kind enough to ask me for several days each season (only so he can enjoy the pleasure of being beastly to me) I ask him to my little shoot at Hauxton for as many days as he can manage. The differing scales of our respective shoots are extreme and that point is not lost on him. So, recently when I went to his shoot he suggested a fair way of reciprocating hospitality. As he had had nine shots in the morning at Hauxton I could have nine shots at the first drive at his shoot where I was to be shooting later that week and twenty-four shots in the second drive, equating to what he had fired in the afternoon. I tried to negotiate an acreage adjustment without success.

So, come the day I drew peg number four – right in the middle of the line at the Weasenham Belt, a great drive. Next to me Barry hopped about with anticipation of my frustration as he was on peg number five. The first partridge appeared straight to me. 'One shot, eight to go', he shouted.

Then others came but actually split on me so I could only realistically get one from the edge of the covey. Then a jay made a bad career move. Barry spent more time counting my shots than focusing on his birds. The pheasants started to come and actually they too split, but I had three with my last three shots before painfully putting my gun in its slip. There was a lull – then Nick the keeper, blew the horn. The drive was over.

Barry just could not believe it. I had popped nine head of game in the bag with my quota of shots and then no more birds came to tease me, which left him far more frustrated than me – even more so having spent the drive counting my shots at the expense of his own opportunities. He had leant across and shot a couple of my birds but, without a hint of guilt, said they were all his birds anyway. I suppose there is no argument to that.

His ploy on the second drive was no better as the partridges flushed in one large cloud and after a rattle of shots it was all over. The rest of the day I had no limits and lots of sport. A magic draw ensured that whatever Barry tried it did not stop birds coming to me. Even when I was peg number one at the main drive (having been dispatched out to peg minus two, a hundred yards from my nearest gun), I still picked eleven birds which had obviously lost their sense of direction and flown out into open country.

There was one very happy day for him a year or two ago, when I was not at my best and fighting off some bug. Then one barrel of my gun failed at the beginning of the big drive and I shot poorly with the one still functioning. Barry's smiley face was a picture as with tears of ecstatic joy he came over after the drive to sarcastically ask if I'd enjoyed it.

What are friends for if not to have fun together? Our continued badinage can only come out of good friendship and mutual respect – or am I kidding myself? The sad truth for Barry is that I really enjoy days shooting with him because, or in spite, of his intentions. At tea after the shoot he did quieten for a moment on hearing that I felt an article coming on. Is there not a saying – something about the power of the pen being mightier than. . .?

It won't work in this case, as Barry's humour is sharper than any sword. I will probably live to regret sharing this story with you.

The Ultimate Safari

I awoke at dawn as a million honey bees hummed amongst the flowers of the acacia trees surrounding the glade in which our mobile camp was set. All was remarkably civilised: in fact, as Longusi, my Masai tent boy poured morning tea, I realised that the dawn till dusk safari experience was very spoiling.

This was an adventure of a lifetime, combining the most exciting bird shooting with big game viewing in northern Kenya. The original scheme was a safari to raise funds for the Countryside Alliance, provided by four benefactors who organise everything involved in African safari travel and sport. These included The Ultimate Travel Company, specialists in top quality world sporting travel led by Martin Thompson; Ker & Downey, exclusive safari and bird shooting operators led by Henry Henley; Pierres Bastard of Acacia Trails Ltd, for the most sensational sandgrouse shooting and Tropic Air who flew the party between camps. This amazing trip was the star lot of a Countryside Alliance auction and Ian Wills, our party leader, was the generous successful bidder.

INTO THE DESERT

It was a party of Ian's friends and their wives who emerged from spacious twin-bedded tents with ensuite safari bathrooms into the bright rays of the morning sun, accompanied by the music of a rich cacophony of the African 'dawn chorus'. Was this reality or were we just dreaming? After breakfast we were ready for an early morning drive to view game on the Lewa Downs conservancy.

Henry Henley, together with Nigel Dundas and Derek Dames, two other top Ker & Downey guides, drove the three purpose-built safari vehicles. Perched on the top of each was an African spotter. These men have the eyesight of raptors and from a moving vehicle can see the flick of a kudu's ear in the shade of a thicket half a mile away.

The knowledge shared by Henry, Derek and Nigel was so interesting, not just about the animals but birds, plants and trees as well as tribal cultures and all things African. Elephants mingled in family groups beneath the shade of acacias; black rhinos, armour-plated, stood as solid as the rocks; giraffes arched their necks to delicately nibble the tops of thorny trees. All these animals were at peace with their world and at times were so close you could feel them with all your senses. Twenty years ago however, so many of Kenya's animals had been persecuted or poached to extinction. This followed a ban on hunting in 1976 prior to which hunter, hunted and man co-existed, each with respect for the others' existence.

At the time of the ban there were 20,000 rhinos, however within eight years nearly every rhino had been slaughtered.

One man's vision has helped to reverse this catastrophe. That man, Ian Craig, has achieved this at Lewa Downs by converting his successful 55,000 acre cattle ranch, comprising open and wooded grassy plains, steep river valleys and rocky outcrops and hillsides, into a sanctuary. This is known today as the Lewa Wildlife Conservancy. The success of Lewa has become the springboard for an inspired project to establish further conservancies in northern Kenya. Now some twelve areas are in the scheme known as the Northern Rangelands Trust Community Project. It improves the livelihoods of communities through conservation and biodiversity on their land which symbiotically produces the successful balance between nature and man. It is funded by safaris and bird shooting, and managed to benefit all.

LOOKING FOR QUAIL

At Lewa we must have seen thirty species of mammals, and the wonderful bird life would make a birding safari on its own. Wherever we drove there were sights or sounds of beauty and interest.

In mid-afternoon we set off to walk-up quail. After a short drive beyond the Lewa Conservancy we climbed up out of the valley along a track seldom used. The Masai beaters used machetes to hack down thorny branches which obstructed the way; others removed rocks that littered the track. Wherever we were going, I certainly felt it was 'first time over'! We stopped on the plain above the valley where a waist-high plant with prickly burrs grew in wide glades. It was good advice to bring tough shooting spats. Harlequin quail, birds the size of jack snipe, buzzed low but fast, making for spontaneous and challenging shooting.

The line of eight Guns interspersed with Masai beaters stopped when a bird was being picked. The testing targets meant a bag was hard earned though we saw plenty of birds. Additions to the bag were doves which occasionally flittered overhead from any direction or between the bushes amongst the quail cover. The distant snow-topped Mount Kenya could be seen above the hills and, as we counted the bag, the setting sun silhouetted the Masai beaters perched on the tops of the vehicles.

IN THE SKY AT NIGHT

Back in camp, after a shower and change we gathered for drinks around the campfire. Above us the African sky was infinite and yet so embracing as we were held in the brilliance of a million stars looking down on us, so small and transitory, in a universe and continent so ancient. It was becoming a week in which we were in a spell like lovers, not in the real world but for that moment so perfect.

Jessica, Henry's wife and Mara, Martin's daughter were our hostesses and organisers of the most delicious food. The skills of the camp staff to achieve this with fairly primitive charcoal ovens and hot beds on which to boil, fry and grill meant every dish was enhanced by the essence of the trees around us.

The following day we set off in the cool of the morning and had another even more successful quail and dove shoot. In a normal year the rich experience and variety of the quarry would have included francolin and yellow-neck spurwing with guinea fowl drives across the valleys. However, late rains the previous December caused a flush of vegetation and these species were nesting at the time of our visit in late February and so were off our sporting menu.

However, Pierres Bastard welcomed us to an extra day at his fly camp at Melaku, a fifty-minute flight north of Lewa. We flew over an arid landscape where we could see small flocks of goats being tended by boys of the local tribe. This was mankind on the edge of survival.

So different however was the camp when we arrived, under trees on the bank of a dry river bed. The view was of cattle, sheep, goats and camels being brought to drink from holes where plentiful water was just below the surface of the sand.

CHALLENGING SPORT

That evening we were in for an extreme shooting challenge. For an hour prior to this we shot intermittent late visitors to the open water along a half mile of river bed. These were chestnut-bellied and black-faced sandgrouse together with speckled pigeon. All made interesting shots but at 6.55 p.m. for only fifteen minutes we experienced the most testing shooting as the Lichtenstein sandgrouse flighted in and darkness fell. The little birds appeared out of the gloaming like bats chasing insects and descending like miniature teal at dusk. One moment they were visible against the last orange glow of the western sky and then in a flash they were lost in the darkness. We were proud to shoot twenty-seven of these, apparently it was a record.

Next morning, we were stood along another length of rivulette where the chestnut-bellied and black-faced sandgrouse flighted in great numbers an hour after dawn to drink. We were very excited at this prospect and my gunbearer Singudi, a 6 foot 7 inch fine figure of a man from the Rendille local tribe, set up my seat and gun. The first birds appeared, a covey high from the east, then a few single birds, before larger groups.

Soon we were all having shooting as we selected the most sporting shots and our bird boys scampered about retrieving. Each gun had an allocation of a hundred cartridges. Quite right, as these are numerous but very special birds. We could enjoy a lot of shooting yet select sandgrouse of all heights, speeds or angles but equally have time to stand in awe of the spectacle, as at times inestimable numbers of birds filled the sky. After a shot they accelerated and exploded in all directions before flying further downriver to drink in the areas left undisturbed. In this way, of the estimated fifteen thousand, none but the 235 in the bag was deprived of a vital drink.

Brunch was followed by a siesta in the heat of the day, 39 °C in the shade, before enjoying the same evening and morning flights at different water holes. Further opportunities to augment one's thrill of these little torpedo-shaped birds with sickle-shaped wings built for speed. We then flew back to Lewa which, at an altitude of 5,000 feet is higher than Melaku and so the temperature is cooler, in fact very pleasant.

REMEMBERING KENYA

Next afternoon four of us went to investigate dusky dove shooting on the high altitude (9,000 ft) arable farmland in the foothills of Mount Kenya. Harvesting had not yet started so we were too early for great success but shot enough to see the quality of the bird and experience yet another variety of sport.

As with any gathering of kindred spirits the trip was full of meaningful or amusing moments as well as other surreal ones. Two in particular come to mind which seemed to bring a smile. Ian in a brand new pair of green wellies in the sand desert scrub or Ali with a hot-water bottle fetish as we camped within a lion's roar of the equator. Philip of Farr may set a new trend for Scottish lairds to abandon their Purdeys for Czechoslovakian over-unders, such was his success with one.

There were a number of notable observations of the whole trip. Firstly how suited it was for the great enjoyment of both husbands and wives. It was not just a jolly for shooting chaps but, with all the game viewing, horse riding, birding and great comfort of the camps, the girls loved it. Also, it felt very safe without snakes or insects waiting with evil intent. In fact it would be suitable for families or anyone from nine to ninety years old, of either sex.

The bird shooting is not only managed to be totally sustainable but as more areas develop by the example of the Northern Rangeland Community Schemes, so many more opportunities will open up for safaris and bird shooting. In a way our party were pioneers of what is sure to become the greatest African safari holiday and a new shooting experience of the future.

Acknowledgements

First I would like to acknowledge Mike Barnes for, albeit by mistake, getting me involved in writing for the *Shooting Gazette* fifteen years ago when he was the editor. I am therefore also very grateful to him for writing the Foreword to this book. It is appropriate that he should make this contribution which completes the circle of the coming together of this anthology.

Second, I must thank the various editors of the magazine over the years for their patience with my handwriting, from which they have worked creatively to make sense of my scribblings. A particular thanks to Will Hetherington, the present editor and his assistant editor Martin Puddifer who is the unfortunate one who now actually edits the articles.

Finally, thanks to Andrew Johnston and his good team at Quiller Publishing who have produced this book. Thanks particularly to Gail Dixon-Smith for editing and Martin Diggle for proof reading; both had an encouraging empathy with the spirit of my stories and contributed positively to the result.